Introducing Islam from Within

Alternative Perspectives

MONA ABUL-FADL

The Islamic Foundation

ISBN 0 86037 209 X (Paperback)
ISBN 0 86037 208 1 (Hardback)

Published by
The Islamic Foundation,
Markfield Dawah Centre,
Ratby Lane,
Markfield,
Leicester LE6 0RN,
United Kingdom

Quran House,
P.O. Box 30611,
Nairobi,
Kenya

P.M.B. 3193,
Kano,
Nigeria

British Library Cataloguing in Publication Data

Abul-Fadl, Mona
Introducing Islam from Within: alternative perspectives.
I. Title
297

ISBN 0-86037-208-1
ISBN 0-86037-209-X

Printed and bound by
Cromwell Press Ltd., Broughton Gifford, Wiltshire

بسم الله الرحمن الرحيم

Contents

Contents

Acknowledgements

I would like to thank all those who have helped in one way or another in the production of this work. Jerry Bookin-Weiner was Director of the Center of International Programs at Old Dominion University at the time it was first launched and he provided me with access to technical facilities. Phillip Gillette showed an enlightened interest in my work and provided much appreciated moral support when it was needed. Later, Bob Crane read through an earlier draft and made some helpful suggestions which stimulated me to rewriting chapter four. Most of all, I am indebted to my mother, Doctor Zahira Hafez Abdin, whose idea and hope it was to see this modest piece of work receive the widest circulation possible. Taking precious time off a congested schedule, and diverting her mind from far more engrossing preoccupations, she read through the essays and was convinced that they had something of value to offer where it was most needed.

Indeed, that was the very spirit which had animated the effort from the outset. Inspired by a sense of duty and responsibility, I was driven to share my knowledge, when called upon, with those who sought to find out what Islam was about, how Muslims related to it and how it affects their lives today. If I have been able to communicate some of that light to others, then *alhamdulillah,* praise God, for enabling me to do so. For my failings and lapses, may He forgive and instruct me as He is evermost the All-Compassionate, the All-Forgiving, the Source of all our knowledge and the Just End to all our strivings.

I would also like to express my gratitude and appreciation to The Islamic Foundation who have made it possible for this manuscript to see the light of day. May God reward all those who live up to their trust.

Mona Abul-Fadl

Foreword

The purpose of the present volume is to promote a better understanding of Islam and to develop some insights into the Faith as it is perceived and lived by Muslims. *Introducing Islam from Within: Alternative Perspectives* is a series of essays originally written to supplement the basic reading requirements and outreach material used in a course for Public School Teachers in the Norfolk and Virginia Beach areas on the East Coast in the United States. The Course, conducted between 13th February and 20th March 1985, was designed to introduce participants to Islam and the Middle East. As Foreign Curriculum Consultant for the academic year 1984–85 at the Center sponsoring the Course, the Center for International Programs at Old Dominion University, I was invited to participate as resource person and discussant. The effective class situation left little room to respond fully to questions raised there. Nor was it possible to bring in adequately the insight and commentary that I felt that my position as discussant called for. To overcome this sense of frustration, I took to drafting my observations and comments in the form of additional notes to be circulated among participants as the Course progressed. The upshot of this effort was this series that tended to be self-complementary, combining to provide an overall picture of Islam as a living Faith that has its relevant social and political implications for the world we live in today.

The essays are presented here essentially as they were originally drafted. They are deemed to bring a missing dimension to the material that is commonly available to the average reader on Islam in the United States. This dimension is described in the title as 'Introducing Islam from Within'. Its purpose is to convey to those outside the cultural pale of Islam the world-view, self-understanding and concepts of the average cultured and practising Muslim. As an intellectual, my role here was simply to exercise a measure of analytical self-awareness and try to articulate this experience and communicate it to others. The range and depth of this experience draws on the wealth, breadth and intensity of Islam, the Faith, itself. To articulate an experience may be difficult in itself; to communicate it to others is a challenge that brings its own reward. Packed with ideas that are often interrelated and abstract, it is hoped that many of the paragraphs which follow will invite the reader's attention, and that the level at which the inside dimension of Islam is explored here will be such as to stimulate his interest, without unduly taxing his concentration. The 'prelude', which precedes each essay and links the one to the other, has been added to quicken the sensibility and to orient the reader to an inspired and inspiring comprehension of what follows.

The immediate target is not the High School students themselves, at least not directly so. Rather, it is directed at an interested and qualified audience – in the sense that it assumes some basic knowledge of Islam and its history. Such an audience includes those teachers whose courses touch on Islam, whether their field is World Geography, History, World Civilization or Sociology, as well as those teaching more specialized courses on the Middle East or on World Religion. In assimilating the material presented here, it is hoped that the teacher may acquire an added sensibility that will enhance his or her skills at communicating with their students in a field that remains generally unfamiliar and remote to their common world alike. To help the teacher obtain the greatest benefit from this material, it is suggested that he or she should proceed to break it down into its 'constituents' and make summary charts that relate the different ideas and sequences to one another. Here, the basic format should be helpful. The sequence of Preludes that anticipate core ideas, or highlight the thrust of the presentation that follows may provide a practical organizing focus in this respect.

The Qur'ān is in Arabic, the original language of its revelation and transmission. I have therefore deliberately used or introduced Arabic/Islamic terms wherever possible. To facilitate reference, or retention, I have included a simple glossary. However, throughout the condensed and closely reasoned paragraphs articulating fundamental precepts and relating concepts to one another, direct citing from the Qur'ān has been minimal. To make good this omission, a selective thematic review of 'Islam from its Sources' has been added as an Appendix. It is presented here merely as a start and a stimulus for seeking out the Qur'ān and trying to follow up this compilation. For those who may be interested to find out more about Islam, some further reading is suggested. The selection has typically been made with an eye to reinforcing the 'inside dimension' – for this is seen to be most needed by outsiders – especially when they are unfamiliar with the language of the original. Also included as Appendices are two excerpts: one on how the Qur'ān, the Holy Book of Islam, came to be authenticated and collected; the other, an essay – 'On Being Muslim' – is given as an example of how close a non-Muslim can develop an empathy for his subject. Because the spirit in which this whole project is conceived is one of promoting an intra-cultural understanding, this practical instance of 'bridge-crossing' is particularly heartening.

Presenting Islam in terms of concepts and ideals that impregnate the texture of society and infuse the historically real poses a difficulty in view of the abstraction it entails. To counter this, and to render a more vivid dimension to the written text, I have devised a visual presentation to accompany it. It is designed to familiarize the viewer with the world-view of Islam in such a manner that the conceptual and the intellectual are reinforced with the perceptual and the tangible. A slide kit including over 200 slides together with a set of orienting notes addresses six distinct and related themes under the title of *Islamopax, Islamolites: the Peace of Islam, the Light of Islam.* In addition to the title theme, others include the following: 'The Universe: From Astrolabe to Astrolites', 'The Cosmic Bond: Rites and Concordances', 'The Community: From Niche to Sanctuary', 'Visual Harmonics', 'The Human Setting'; and 'The Word: its Power and Ubiquity'. In the initial piloting of this project this supplementary visual segment was well received. It has been successfully used to enlighten as it entertains; to break a monotony or dilute an idea, at the same time as it instructs in a congenial medium geared to a more effective communication of values and ideas across the cultural spectrum. I hope to make it eventually available for a wider circulation as an integral component and a vital and original contribution to the present reading of *Islam from Within.*

Herndon, Virginia
November 1988

Mona Abul-Fadl

ALLAH IS THE LIGHT OF THE HEAVENS
AND OF THE EARTH
THE PARABLE OF HIS LIGHT IS AS IT WERE
A NICHE AND WITHIN IT A LAMP:
THE LAMP ENCLOSED IN GLASS:
THE GLASS IN THE LIKENESS OF
A GLITTERING PLANET
KINDLED FROM A BLESSED TREE
AN OLIVE – NEITHER OF THE EAST
NOR OF THE WEST –
WHOSE OIL WELL NIGH GLOWS FORTH
THOUGH NO FIRE SCARCE TOUCHES IT:
LIGHT UPON LIGHT –
ALLAH GUIDES TO HIS LIGHT
WHOM HE WILLS:
ALLAH SETS FORTH PARABLES FOR HUMANKIND;
ALLAH IS ALL-KNOWING,
COMPREHENDS ALL THINGS

(24: 35)

CHAPTER 1

The Meaning of Islam: Tawḥīd and Related Concepts

Prelude

Monotheism – the belief in the One God to the exclusion of any other deity, and 'monotheism', in the sense of the denial of the attributes of divinity to any power other than the One and Only God is what the Pure Religion is all about. This is also the substance of tawḥīd. *The Pure Religion is not something man stumbled across by chance, after a sequence of trial and tribulation, nor is the Pure Religion a preserve of any one people in history to the exclusion of others, or a gift of one race to the rest of humanity. The Pure Religion comes as a gift of Guidance that is dispensed in bountiful mercy to all men alike. Its Source is the One and Only God who elects from among His creation messengers to bring the good tidings, to warn, to admonish, to inform, to instruct and to guide to the light of Righteousness whoever chooses to respond to the Guidance. Just as the source of the Pure Religion is one, so too is the substance of its message one and the same. The name of that Religion which all the Messengers carried and the true Prophets preached, from Adam through Noah and from Abraham through Moses and Jesus to Muḥammad was the archetype of 'the one who surrenders himself to God in a spirit of devoted and single-minded commitment to His Will' which is the literal meaning of the term 'Muslim'. His progeny among the nations who were entrusted with the Divine Mission were all Muslims and preached Islam (2: 130–6; 3: 84–5). The last of these Messages came to be recorded verbatim as it was revealed from its Source and it came to be preserved as such. It confirmed the truth of that which had gone before, removed the human accretions that blurred and confused, and completed and perfected the Pure Religion.*

The name Islam *thus came to be institutionalized in the recorded history of man with the last of the Messages. It came to be identified with a universal community that from its outset hailed from all origins and races. This community converged round a common bond of Faith, shared in its world history, aspirations and destiny. It was a community whose members modelled themselves on the human example of its founder and leader, the Prophet and Messenger (peace be upon him) and a community that sought its precedents in the actions and situations of that formative period. It continued to draw its inspiration and seek its practical guidance from the 'Recitation' that was revealed to Muḥammad (peace be upon him). This is the* Umma, *or the Community, that became the repository of the Pure Religion. It sees itself as the* ummat al-tawḥīd *– or the Community of Monotheism. This latter is the core and nucleus of an open universal community that is potentially co-extensive with humanity in its entirety.*

The following essay confines itself to aspects of the Faith of which this Community is the repository, rather than to the Community itself. The following are some of the questions addressed:

- *What are the different meanings of the term 'Islam' – and how are they related to one another?*
- *What is* Tawḥīd? *What are its practical consequences?*
- *More explicitly, what is the world-view that* tawḥīd *as a doctrine promotes?*
- *What are the key concepts that go into the making of that comprehensive world-view?*
- *What does the term 'religion' mean? What does 'devotion' or 'worship' mean? What is the purpose of creation? What does the concept of man's vicegerency* (khilāfa) *convey? (i.e. Elements of the world-view).*
- *By virtue of the interrelationship of the family of concepts that grow from* tawḥīd, *man's worldly life is transformed into a 'devotional grid'. How well do you think this expression conveys the meaning of Islam?*

The purpose of this presentation is to explore one of the many dimensions inherent in the meaning of Islam. This dimension will take the etymological, or root-meaning of the term 'Islam', within a restricted context, in order to illustrate a key concordance between the 'idea' and the 'form', the belief-system and the way of life. Underlying this demonstration is the conviction that Islam provides man with a comprehensive world-view that is rooted in a coherent system of ideas and beliefs that together impart a strength and consistency, a logic and vitality to the Faith. By taking tawḥīd *the Islamic monotheistic principle, as a core-principle in that belief-system, the distinct and complementary aspects of the meaning of Islam are related to it and, in the process, they are related to each other. In the process too, other Islamic terms and concepts are briefly explained and duly located in the context of the whole. In this way it is hoped that some insight into certain aspects that contribute to the uniqueness of Islam among world religions may be gained.*

Islam is the *dīn* (pronounced as *deen)* chosen by God for man. *'Dīn'* is man's response to his Creator. *'Dīn'* means: allegiance, judgement, debt, account, way of life. Islam means submitting to the Will of the One and Only God, Allah: the total self-surrender to the Lord of the Worlds, *rabb al-'ālamīn.* Islam also derives from the root word for Peace: S-L-M. The coherence of the central belief-system in Islam is based on the relationship between the act of submission and its consequences in a state of peace. Peace has both an outer dimension, in security, and an inner dimension in a tranquillity, or a serenity (*sakīna* and in the former: *amn* or, *amān*). At the core of this relationship is the concept of *tawḥīd* by virtue of which submission is transformed into a dynamic and ongoing act that assumes the dimensions of totality, exclusiveness and comprehensiveness. This is the meaning of *'ibāda* (devotion, worship). It begins by an active commitment to pledge one's being to the fulfilment of the Will of God in all one undertakes. The foremost quality of mind and character that flows from this commitment is a state of constant vigilance, or an awareness, of the presence of God, the All-Knowing. It is this quality of God-Consciousness *(taqwā)* which is at the heart of the traits cultivated by the basic duties in Islam (the *arkān*: corners, or Pillars).

From voluntarily bowing one's will to the Will of one's Creator, to the vigilant commitment to upholding that Will, the Way of Peace, both inner and outer is assured by yet two other conditions. On the one hand, *tawḥīd* ensures the exclusiveness of the bond of allegiance. Muslims bow to One Lord Alone to Whom is owed loyalty to the exclusion of all else. In this way the question of dual and conflicting loyalties does not arise and the command lines are clear: the Muslim always has one and only one ultimate point of reference for deciding on right and wrong, on Truth and Justice. With this ultimate allegiance and point of reference everything that *is* becomes relative, all worldly powers are relativized and all human relations are seen to have value only to the extent that they can relate to that ultimate referent. This whole attitude is encapsulated and condensed in the simple but categorical affirmation: *Allāhu Akbar!* This is diversely rendered in English as God is Great, God is Greater, and God is Greatest. The fact that in Arabic there are only two conditions, the simple and the comparative, lends itself admirably to the idea expressed. The fact that God is Great is beyond question. To say that God is the Greatest carries with it derogatory insinuations that there could be a question of competing candidates for greatness, or the heretic connotations of associating any other in the attributes of divinity. In the simple comparative the comparison itself carries with it the note of being both exclusive and absolute – both elements in the core concept of *tawḥīd*. Furthermore, in addition to ruling out the strains and the confusion arising out of divided loyalties, *tawḥīd* also resolves the issue of divided attention and 'wasted' or dissipated energy. For the undivided allegiance subsumes the breadth of the Muslim's devotion. There is no division between the 'sacred' and the 'profane' – as the whole span of the Muslim's life is sanctified by the nature of his pledge to his Creator. In effect, the Muslim's entire being is integrated round the One Way and the Ultimate End.

These ideas and beliefs are of practical import to the extent that they condition an attitude and outlook to existence and find an expression in the actual conduct of a way of life. In this way, the meaning of Islam becomes a subject of practical content – not of philosophical speculation. With this remark, we shall continue to draw on the above implications.

Peace and integration are not only ends for which human beings strive, but they are also conditions for fulfilling the purpose of human existence on earth. In the first instance, *tawḥīd* provides the Way, in the second, *tawḥīd* prescribes that purpose, which in fact flows from it and is encompassed by it. The act of singling out for exclusive allegiance and total devotion the One True God constitutes the starting point for all subsequent human activity and remains at its very core. As life by definition negates 'stasis' and confirms action, whether it be in that state of being or in the process of becoming, motion is another of the cardinal principles of Creation. Consistent with this principle, human beings are inherently active beings, oriented towards a state of activity. Man is a born achiever, yet, the nature of that achievement must not be assumed but investigated. Will man use his active energy to build or to destroy? Will he strive to achieve glory or will he glorify in infamy? It is here, in this context, that the state of inner peace, along with the sense of proportion and integration it comprehends, will come to influence one's response to the human condition and to determine whether one is to project one's being creatively or otherwise.

Against this background, it is clear that a balanced psyche and an integrated being are necessary for a constructive existence. A constructive existence is positively disposed toward its environment. It avails itself with just measure of the resources at its command, the bounties created by God and put at the disposal of man to use, (the concept of *taskhīr*) not to abuse, to dispose of the physical and natural environment, not to violate it. Construction, edification and civilization are, in the perspective of *tawḥīd,* tasks for which Adam was originally created (concept of *khilāfa*). God equipped him for this task with the faculties needed, provided the resources and authorized the mission. He also provided the guidelines for the Way (the Guidance: *al-hudā*). For the edification to be noble, it must be in the direction that complies with the Will and Command of God. This constitutes the *amāna* or the Trust, for which Adam was the nominated trustee. As a result, a Muslim, by virtue of his submission in *tawḥīd* is committed to a lifetime of striving in the Way of God: a striving in constancy and perseverance to 'enjoin the Good and forbid the Wrong', and altogether to fulfil the purpose of his creation. This engages him in combating, fighting off, the corrupting influences that undermine, or impede the edification in the Noble Way. Islam, the bowing to the Will of God, the Way of Peace through complying with the Laws of Creation, is transformed in the world of free, active and mortal human beings into a dynamic code of moral responsibility and a just striving *(jihād)*. This is the code subsumed under the notion of *'ibāda* or devotion and worship. It constitutes an all-encompassing activity that is the fibre and fabric of the Muslim's life.

To recapitulate on the above. In pledging allegiance to One Master, the range of one's being becomes subject to One Command and falls within that Unique jurisdiction. Not only is a Muslim spared the conflict of divided loyalty, but he is assured the reward of whatever he undertakes. Since the pledge in *tawḥīd* has transformed the scope of active existence, of self-exertion and striving in worldly life into a fertile expanse of devotion, the most ordinary of tasks is promoted from a distraction and a waste or dissipation, into an aspect of the Muslim's devotion. The implications of this attitude for a sound individual psyche and for a creative potential in the community at large are naturally immense. It means the resolution of tensions that are inherent in the human condition and are otherwise unresolvable. The spiritual is reconciled to the physical, freedom to authority, worldly concerns to the Hereafter in a sequence that structures and integrates the life of the believer round a unified and unifying core nucleus expressed in *tawḥīd*. It is the state of inner peace that flows from this wholeness of self and soundness of heart that releases the creative impulse and potential energies and harnesses them in a given Way – 'the straight path' – towards a determined and sure, unfailing and certain notion (*wajh 'Allāh*). The Muslim's life, to the extent that it is lived in a state of self-awareness, and its corollary, that state of God-consciousness, becomes the unfolding record of a process of purposeful and single-minded devotion.

The basic rites referred to in accordance with the tradition as the 'pillars of the faith', *arkān al-dīn,* are all geared to the nourishment and the strengthening of that moral fibre. They constitute the devotions, in the narrower and more literal sense of the term, and as such are part of the more comprehensive notion referred to above – a notion which is co-extensive with life and an activity of a lifetime itself. The formal rituals are themselves symbolic of an embodiment for this way of life. Consider that prime of symbols, the Ka'ba, which provides the *qibla* or the pointer and direction for the Way, and consider the rituals associated with it in a general way, and which are manifest in the *ḥajj* in particular, like *ṭawāf*. The Ka'ba is the symbolic centre and core of *tawḥīd*. It constitutes the *qibla* to which all Muslims gravitate – or orient themselves – in all their devotions and actions (whence, the symbolism of the ritual prayer itself). When Muslims are physically brought into its presence, or its precincts, they cannot but tune into a Universal Cosmic law inscribed by the Creator for all of Creation, and prescribed by way of rite for man. It is the law of circumrotation. As the Muslim voluntarily submits to his Creator he follows in the prescribed way and partakes of the majestic order. The Ka'ba becomes the visible focus, and the tangible centre for this majestic demonstration of 'Islam' the act and the meaning, as the Muslims gravitate towards the centre of their being and orbit the symbolic *bait ullāh* 'House of God'. In their devotion, the pilgrims become spiralling human clusters – of dust and light – reduced to their basic elements, as they vibrate into orbit, and come to blend beautifully with and dissolve into a vast cosmic harmony that encompasses all of creation from the atom to the galaxies. The Way of Peace culminates in the convergence of the physical and the spiritual in the Universe. In Islam, the Response by man to his Creator; and in Islam, the Way chosen by God for man, this convergence is complete.

A Muslim's life is like a global grid that is intersected at regular intervals by the specific injunctions and diverse commands of his Faith. In the web of the ensuing relations, transactions and interactions that make the span of his worldly life, it is these intersections that come to lend a coherence and meaning to the whole. The global grid turns out to be nothing other than a devotional grid. The life of the Muslim comes into perfect focus with the Will of his Creator – and ultimate Refuge – on a note of sublime concord and harmony. The Divine Injunction: 'I have not created man and jinn except that they should serve Me in pure devotion (or: worship Me)' (51: 56) is fulfilled in the devout response on the part of the believer: 'Say: Truly my prayers and my rites (devotions), my life and my death are (consecrated in their entirety) to Allah (Alone), Lord of the Worlds' (6: 16). If *tawḥīd* is the core, 'Islam', the bowing of the will in submission to its Creator, was the source and the Way that inspired it. Again, with *tawḥīd* at the core, 'Islam' (S-L-M), the true peace was the yield and fruit that resulted from it. In this way, it is possible to appreciate the impact of Islam on the human condition, in all its diversity, complexity and multi-faceted dimension – as a powerful integrator that is all-encompassing and ever-expanding.

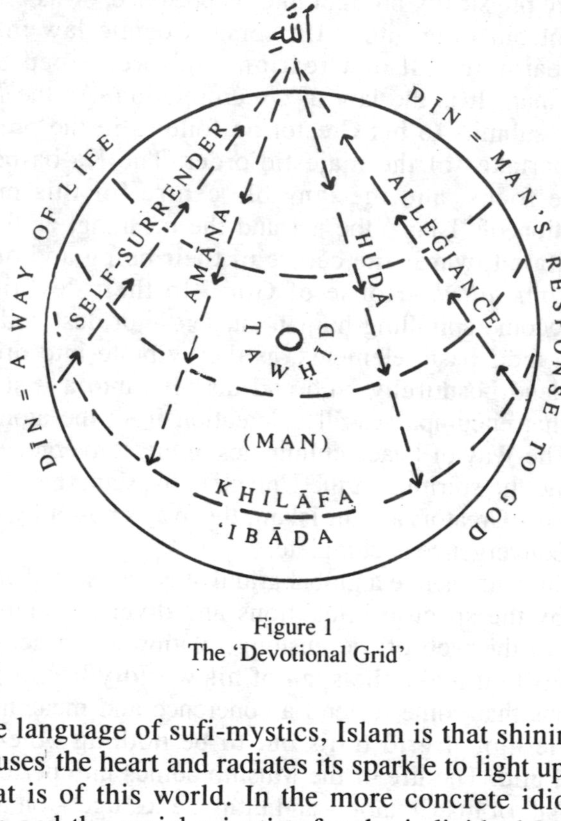

Figure 1
The 'Devotional Grid'

In the language of sufi-mystics, Islam is that shining crystal that infuses the heart and radiates its sparkle to light up the darkness that is of this world. In the more concrete idiom of the historian and the social scientist, for the individual Muslim and for the corporate community, Islam constitutes that bond of devotion and that life-binding pledge which assures both cohesion and coherence to historical existence. It guides peoples and individuals in the Way of Truth, Peace and Justice – which is ultimately one integral way. For Truth, Peace and Justice are among the Beautiful Names of Allah *(al-asmā' al-ḥusnā)* (20: 8).

In Islam there is no dogma in the sense that there is no intricate doctrine beyond human reason that must be taken at face value, never to be questioned. The cornerstone of the Faith expressed in *tawḥīd* is explicit, clear, and simple. In the Qur'ān there are no brain-boggling formulas. There are however teachings about the Faith revealed through the Qur'ān in a tenor that is clear, direct, open and conclusive. There is no ambiguity. These are the teachings regarding Islam as the Only Way, the only *dīn* acceptable to God (3: 19, 83–5) and that because it is the only *dīn* that has been prescribed by Him for mankind (5: 3; 61: 9) the warning that no other response from us human beings is acceptable to God; the Good Tidings that whosoever earnestly sets out to seek God and whomever God chooses to favour will be granted Mercy. God will inspire the heart of the truthful to expand and open up to receive the Light and Guidance of Islam (6: 125; 39: 22). Last but not least, the teachings in the Qur'ān reveal the assurance and the Grace that the Guidance of God to us has been completed and perfected with the advent of the Final Prophet (peace be upon him) and that henceforth to the end of time, it will be preserved intact in a Book that will be accessible to all who seek it, and that this Book will be immune to loss, or to human accretions and the contaminations of time. God Almighty who revealed it will Himself watch over it and protect it (15: 9; cf. also 18: 109).

The Grace of this assurance came towards the end of the Mission of the Messenger of God, *Rasūl Allāh* (peace be upon him), over twenty-two years after the first *āya* (Verse, Sign) was revealed. That had proclaimed the start of the Recitation, the Holy Reading (96: 1). Meanwhile, between the earliest and the last Revelation which was sent down from On High, the *tanzīl*, the Messenger of God (peace be upon him) had led a life of arduous struggle, in the Way of the Message and the Mission, and was subject to all the perils that befall a mortal existence. Indeed, in one of the earlier battles fought in the first years of the *Hijra* (the Emigration to Madina) he was severely wounded and rumour circulated of his death. But for all his mortality, Muḥammad (peace be upon him), was chosen by Allah for a mission that was to be completed, and He who giveth life and taketh life away, preserved His Chosen One, until the mission was perfected. This is why, in his utterances, the beloved Prophet was, without doubt, invariably inspired (53: 2–5). The *āya* of the perfection of the *dīn* (5: 3) chronologically, came towards the end to proclaim the completion of the Recitation, that Ultimate and Conclusive Writ of Guidance. Shortly thereafter, in a season of the *ḥajj* following the conquest of Makka the Prophet (peace be upon him) spoke his will and testimony to the Community he was soon to leave behind. It came to be known as the Farewell Sermon. To the very end, the 'Tradition', or the *sunna* of the Prophet, was faithful to its mission as the embodiment of the teachings of the Qur'ān. A few months later, God permitted, and the Servant and Messenger of God (peace be upon him) peacefully succumbed to his mortality.

In one of the most moving accounts recorded by the chroniclers of the *sīra* (the Prophet's biography), the Prophet (peace be upon him) in his address to the jubilant crowds of pilgrims gathered at the foot of Mount 'Arafāt, *Jabal al-Rahma,* had closed his sermon by appealing to them as witnesses in the presence of the Almighty, Himself the Supreme Witness. With a lifetime of struggle in the way of establishing the Message of Truth behind him, he now summed up its core teachings as a testimony and a trust to the Community he was about to leave, and then he called on each of its members: 'Hear, O Hear, have I not proclaimed (my mission to its full) . . . ' Thrice repeated and thrice affirmed, he concluded on the invocation: 'Almighty God, (that this is so, I beseech You) Bear Witness!' *(Allāhuma fashhad!).*

If the Faithful of the times could testify to the truth of the Prophet (peace be upon him) and to his completion of his Mission, the assurance of the preservation of the Guidance was beyond their immediate experience. For them it was an article of Faith. For posterity however, it has become an article of Faith corroborated by historical evidence. Today, fourteen centuries later, believers reap the fruits of this assurance and witness the realization of this Promise as they live among others to see the Record of the Guidance in the Qur'ān stand the test of time in more than a literal sense. For the Muslims as a Community have been subject to all the reversals of fortune that beset other nations as their civilization went into eclipse and their societies degenerated. As peoples, they fell under foreign domination and emerged from the experience weak, divided, backward and struggling to catch up with the times and recover the means to their lost glory. As such, they were in no position to maintain the upswing of their Faith any more than to guard and protect the Repository of that Faith in all its pristine purity. Actually, it is no exaggeration to say that the Qur'ān has been preserved unique, unaltered and intact *despite* the Muslims and more generally, despite and in the face of the many undermining influences to which Islam has been subject. Indeed, while the way of life of the Community itself was contaminated, and historically the *umma* declined, the Qur'ān as the Source of the Faith remained immune to such contamination. Moreover, it continued to retain its relevance as an effective factor of regeneration and renewal whenever the Community recovered its historical consciousness and strove to muster its will to act in history. In fact, it has periodically been at the source of all movements of reform and revival of what we may call a *Kulturgewissen* or a *Kulturwille*.

The vitality of Islam as a Faith may in part, no doubt, be attributed to its unpolluted Source and to the preservation of its 'doctrinal purity'. *Tawḥīd* remains at the heart of the Faith to constitute the force of its appeal and the vigour of its integrationist thrust alike. Variations and divergences within mainstream historic Islam abound, whether in the interpretation of concepts, or in the reaction to situations. What strikes the observer however, is not the differences as much as the underlying threads of consistency and the similarities, that ultimately serve to consolidate the whole and to assert the basic affinity in unity. In a work of refined scholarship, after a close and objective examination of the sources, a modern scholar of Islam emerges with a similar judgement. She puts forward the idea succinctly and eloquently in her conclusion thus:

> Islam begins as a stem, then doubles, then divides into many branches. But the common stem remains, that which holds together all of the differing interpretations and emphases given to it, and this common stem is the recognition of and response to the nature and the will of God.[1]

Not to indulge in eloquence at the expense of clarity, the statement should perhaps be qualified. The 'common stem' is but the unpolluted source of Revelation, the *tanzīl,* itself. The 'numerous branches' are the efforts to interpret and to relate the meaning of

Islam to worldly life. That there is little substantial dispute as to the crucial questions of the Faith, the categorical 'whats' – as with the Nature and the Will of God – is a measure of the Divine Mercy in preserving for humanity the Source of its lucidity and felicity. Beyond that, multiplicity, variety, complementarity, are the order of Creation. The 'hows', the ways and means of relating *tawḥīd* and its family of concepts to an ever-changing and fleeting world constitutes the renewable challenge to the human will to righteousness and to the human capacity of reason in enlightenment. In Qur'ānic terms, it poses a purposeful test of perseverance in *jihād* and *ijtihād*.

Notes and References

1. Jane Smith, *An Historical and Semantic Study of the Term Islam as seen in a sequence of Qur'ān Commentaries,* Harvard Dissertations in Religion 1 (1975); pp. 233–4.

CHAPTER 2

The Pillars of the Faith

Prelude

In answer to the question, 'Instruct us, O Messenger of God, what is meant by "īmān" *(Faith)?' the answer came:* 'Īmān *is that which rests lodged in the heart and is confirmed by the deed.' In Islam, there is no Faith without action; and action which is devoid of the intention (of the Faith) is meaningless in the religious context. To live up to* 'īmān' *in this understanding of it, calls for a certain quality, or presence, in the mind and the heart. This is called* taqwā *which implies a God-fearing, God-heeding, God-loving, God-knowing frame of being, which we will refer to subsequently, as God-*consciousness. *This quality is not an act that is 'observed' once and for all, but is a persistent state of being that can wax and wane, a process of becoming that the believer experiences at all times. The 'five Pillars of the Faith' serve to promote this quality; at the same time their adequate fulfilment is itself a function of this quality of character. The Confession of Faith* (al-shahāda *or the witness*), *regular daily prayers, paying the poor-dues, fasting and making the pilgrimage once in a lifetime – these are commonly referred to as the Five Pillars. They constitute the minimum basic duties incumbent on every Muslim as a believer. Another important purpose of these basic practices is to recall to each and every believer the social or communal dimension of his existence.*

In this essay the following points are made:

(1) There is no 'ritualism' in Islam.

(2) Each of the basic duties is related to the other duties and together these duties combine to impart a common ethos (or ethic) in the community.

(3) The 'spiritual' and the 'physical' are part of an integral

and whole way of life. The practise of the Pillars ensures that this integrated ideal is realized.

(4) The basic duties serve to build up the moral character of both the individual and the community.

(5) The foremost qualities that the observance of these duties promote are God-consciousness and Community-consciousness. Both conduce to a sense of individual accountability – a moral conscience; and social responsibility – a social conscience.

(6) The observance of the basic duties in the spirit that they presuppose and promote, bears consequences both for the individuals that practise them and for the collectivity, or society, in which they are practised.

The question is how does the observance of these duties affect the individual and the community? What is the nature of these practices? How are these practices related to one another and how are they all related to tawḥīd? *In the* ḥadīth, *or sayings of the Prophet (peace be upon him) it is said that Faith is action, and that true religion is that which is reflected in the daily actions and transactions among people* (al-dīn al-mu'āmala). *In what ways do the basic duties of a Muslim contribute to this meaning?*

These are some of the questions the reader should have in mind as he reads through the following pages.

The Confession of Faith: *Al-Shahāda*

The *shahāda* constitutes the first 'pillar' of Islam. It is the conscious bearing of witness to the Absolute Oneness of God, Allah – *subḥānahū wa ta'ālā* (SWT) – and to the fact that Muḥammad (peace be upon him) is His Servant and Messenger. *Tawḥīd* is at the core of *shahāda*. As we have already seen, *tawḥīd* goes beyond the affirmation of The One God to attributing to Him exclusive overlordship and sovereignty over all Creation including our own life in this world. In the creedal formula the affirmation of this absolute Oneness is preceded by a categorical denial of all other deities, that is, of all other ultimate purposes and values, whether power, wealth, prestige or more subtle false gods such as hedonism, dialectical materialism and other such philosophical and ideological 'isms'. Associating any other deities with Allah, or attributing any of the qualities of Divinity and Overlordship to any other human being, or to anything else in His Creation constitutes *shirk.* This is the cardinal sin in Islam for it pollutes the source of the Pure Religion and taints the mind and the heart (4: 48; 22: 31). The binding commitment to the complete submission to the Will of God is predicated on the acknowledgement of the Messenger and message. The commitment to the Faith however, carries with it another far-reaching implication for the Believer.

As the Muslim professes the *shahāda* he also joins the fellowship that subscribes to the Creed and the Way. In relating himself to his Creator, he has simultaneously identified himself to and with his fellow creatures. He acknowledges that there is but One Creator and one humanity. But, above all, he is spiritually elevated from an anonymous member in a disoriented multitude to the rank of Believer and devoted servant, or a Devotee (literally an '*'abdullāh*'). By his conscious and voluntary submission to his Creator, he makes the acknowledgement and takes the Pledge and this earns him membership to a privileged group, the Community of the Devotees, or the *Umma*. The latter is privileged to the extent that its members have committed their lives to the service of God upholding the Good, forbidding the Evil and affirming the Oneness of God (3: 104, 110). This is the meaning of the statement that Islam is Faith and Community. In Islam the individual being gains a Faith as well as an identity. The *shahāda* is the gateway to the Path.

Because of this function of the *shahāda* as a commitment to an allegiance and an identity, it is the only article of the Faith that in its verbal utterance is confined to the first person singular. Subsequently, in all his devotions the Muslim will find himself in the first person plural. He has forfeited his solitude and isolation for the brotherhood of the devotees and the Community (the *Umma*) and only on the Day of Judgement will he be returned to his solitary state again (6: 94). For then he will be called to account before God as an individual in a setting 'where no soul shall bear the burden of another' and 'where each will be assured of what he or she has earned' (6: 164; 16: 97; 40: 40; cf. 74: 38; 16: 96, 111; 3: 30).

The *shahāda* subsumes the belief in the Unseen *(al-ghaib)*. This includes the belief in God, in His Angels, in His Scriptures, in His Messengers and in the Hereafter, which includes the belief in the Day of Judgement. *Al-ghaib* also includes the *qadar,* its good and bad. *Al-qadar* literally means the 'measure' and may be translated as that which has been decreed by God in measure. The acknowledgement of Muḥammad (peace be upon him) as the Messenger of God carries with it a belief in all the Prophets and Messengers who went before him as well as belief in the culmination and summation of the chain of Prophethood with his coming (peace be upon him) as 'the Seal of the Prophets'. The corollary to this belief in the finality of Prophethood is the belief in the Qur'ān, which has been revealed as the verbatim Word of God and preserved as such, to be the final and hence the most complete and perfect message to mankind to serve as Guidance until the End of Time (i.e. the Day of Judgement).

At its simplest therefore the *shahāda* is the acknowledgement of *tawḥīd* by word of mouth and the proclamation of Intent of heart – the *niyya* to pursue in submission the Will and Commands of the One True God. This latter *niyya* is to be sought in observing the letter and the spirit of the Guidance which has been preserved immutable and intact in its Original Source, the Qur'ān. Historically, this Guidance has been mediated in the Traditions of the Prophet (peace be upon him) who thus provides the human exemplar and the model of conduct for the individual believer throughout his life in his various social roles. In this way the *shahāda* is the key to Islam. Islam is about action as well as contemplation and remembrance, *dhikr.* Its ideal is the active, not the passive tense. Its Guidance is for this world, the Here-and-Now in order to benefit the Believer both in this world and the Next. And because all purposeful activity is rooted in intent and motivation, it is primarily concerned with building up the morale and reinforcing the Resolve; it is not just concerned with informing the Mind and orienting the Intent. This then is the joint task of the other Pillars of the Faith. As we shall see they provide both the test and the training ground for forming and promoting the resolve.

Performing Prayers: *Ṣalāt*

This constitutes the 'second pillar' of the Faith. In fact, performing prayers in the prescribed manner and at the set times each day is the first of the practical – testing and training – grounds of Islam. In the Tradition, 'prayer is the cornerstone of *dīn*' – which makes it more than just another 'pillar'. In Islam, the assumption is not that man is sinful, but rather that he is forgetful and weak; he is in need of a constant reminder of his purpose and his goal in life, of his priorities as he goes along, and he is in need of the means to strengthen his will. This is the prime function of prayer in Islam. *Ṣalāt* literally means the connection, the contact. This is why the Tradition states that 'the difference between the believer and the unbeliever lies in maintaining *ṣalāt*'. If the Muslim neglects *ṣalāt,* he has lost the link that keeps him on the Straight Path. He is like the horseback rider who has lost his saddle; he runs the risk of being thrown off at any sharp jerk or lurch of his steed.

The connection maintained through regular prayer is at once a connection with one's Creator and a connection with one's Community/identity. It is moreover, a connection that transcends the individual to the Community and crosses the bounds of space and time. This is true not only of the communal prayer, but of the individual prayer too, on account of its prescribed form and content. And while 'communal' prayer in a formal place of worship, the mosque, is normally obligatory only once a week and on certain occasions, yet group prayer is strongly urged at all times and places, and three is the 'quorum' for a *jamā'a* (a group). In this way, *ṣalāt* simultaneously nourishes the living Faith and cultivates the bonds of Community. It is a daily consecration of *tawḥīd,* the Oneness of God; and of its consequences for the unity and integration of the life of the individual and the community. It also bonds the Community together and impresses upon it its essential unity. Its symbol is the common direction – the *qibla* – which the Muslim orients himself towards and faces, as he stands up, bows and prostrates himself in an all-encompassing act of devotion that synchronizes the mind, heart and body of the devotee in one protracted moment of spiritual, mental and physical exertion.

As in all the other acts of devotion, *ṣalāt* is not an end in itself.

To the extent that concordance is attained between the ritual and the meaning, between the form and the gesture and the mental and the spiritual content, then this Connection has fulfilled its purpose: God-consciousness, *taqwā,* continues to be instilled in the heart, nourished, ingrained and intensified. The test is in the deed, in its active pursuits in this worldly arena. This is why in the call to prayer, the *adhān,* the caller or the muezzin proclaims: 'Come to *Ṣalāt,* Come to the (Way of) Prosperity' – meaning spiritual and worldly prosperity; the measure of the latter is the extent to which the Muslim heeds God in his dealings. In his teachings, the beloved Prophet (peace be upon him) reminds the believer that, 'He whose *ṣalāt* does not restrain from evil and abomination, for him there has been no *ṣalāt*'. In the Qur'ān, *ṣalāt* is explicitly enjoined upon the believer as a means of reinforcing a positive and righteous pattern of conduct (29: 45).

But *ṣalāt* is only one channel, for all its pre-eminence, in training the resolve and inculcating the values of the Faith and in fostering the cohesion of the Community.

The Poor-Dues/Wealth Tax: *Al-Zakāt*

Two primal instincts motivate man's conduct in the realm of material possessions. The first is the instinct to preserve and to increase one's acquisitions, the other is the fear of its loss or diminution. The profit and loss syndrome is behind man's attitude to the accumulation of wealth and his outlook on the exploitation of his environment. The Muslim who has by the *shahāda* acknowledged God's Absolute Oneness, has by the same token acknowledged God's absolute Sovereignty and Lordship; by submitting his will and his whole being to his Master and Sovereign, the devotee concedes in humility, to the noble trusteeship of the wealth (and power) put by his Bountiful Lord, at his disposal. It follows from placing all wealth as a 'trust', that the trustee is accountable for its use and that his freedom is hedged by a calculus of rights and obligations. In principle, the Muslim is entitled to the material acquisitions he has striven for and legitimately earned, subject to a commitment to the overarching ideal of 'trusteeship' – the *amāna.* But this title is confirmed, and the right is sanctified only by allotting out of that acquired wealth a fixed share or portion which is due his

Master. This portion is not a kindness or 'charity' on his part, but a duty to which he is bound in conscience by virtue of his *shahāda*. This is *Zakāt*, the third pillar of Islam.

By relieving himself of his duty to God, the Muslim has 'purified' and 'sanctified' his honest acquisitions. Not only that. But in securing God's blessings on his wealth, the Muslim has thereby assured himself of his own prosperity – again, spiritually, and materially (for by now we can assume that Islam perceives no presumed antagonism, or dissonance between the spiritual and the material). Significantly, the innately human profit-seeking instinct is insured against its own perversion to the detriment of either the individual or the society. There is nothing unholy or perverse about the desire for gain provided it is exercised in the full awareness of the presence of God. It is this devotional setting that guards against the subversion of a natural and commendable instinct into an instrument of avarice and compulsive exploitation.

This is why *Zakāt* can only be translated as '*zakāt*'. For although it is an obligatory and fixed percentage of all wealth and earnings periodically due, it is not just another kind of tax. The distinctiveness of *zakāt* can be seen in the principle underlying its distribution as well as in its fundamental conception. In the absence of a Church that might appropriate to itself the 'share of God', the proceeds go directly to the poor and needy in the Community. Yet, it is more than a 'poor-due'. *Zakāt* connotes 'purification' and 'growth'. Typical of the staple Qur'ānic terminology there is perfect concordance between the form and the substance, or the linguistic etymology and the root meaning, or the substantive concept, it conveys. Just as *ṣalāt* has its roots in the verb 'to connect' or 'to bring together', so too *zakāt* has its root-meaning in the verbs: 'to purify' and 'to grow'.

The Pillars of the Faith are not disparate rites and obligations that stand apart. Rather they are functional to a working and vibrant whole that comprises an integrated moral, social, cultural and spiritual ethos that underlines an integral way of life. So it follows that in any discussion or description of the Pillars they should be interrelated so as to show how, together, they support the structure they command: the Faith and Community.[1] So indeed, we find that just as *ṣalāt* had its individual and its communal repercussions, its inner and outer dimensions for the Faith and the Community, so too with *zakāt* which is not just an act of devotion that serves to bring the Muslim closer to God by testing his will in the domain of wealth and property, but it is simultaneously an act of community. It fosters the bonds of cohesion in a practical way that goes beyond the symbolics of gesture and ritual, though it is not void of symbolism either. Just as the *qibla* in *ṣalāt* embodied Unity as the central organizational value/principle in the fellowship of the Faith, so here too, *zakāt* puts the accent on another major organizational principle/value of Community in Islam: *takāful* (mutual support and mutual responsibility for the welfare of one's brothers).

Again, *zakāt* is but symbolic of an ethos that transcends equality to equity and that transforms Justice from a quantity calculus to a qualitative standard. For justice in Islam is a justice rooted in Mercy and Compassion and not just grounded on Power. Translated to our present context, *zakāt* which subsumes a periodic fixed share of wealth, is but a 'pillar' in a Path that enjoins spending – unsparingly – giving of one's wealth and one's resources in the Way of God – at all times.

This is the concept of *infāq* which is crucial to understanding the meaning of *zakāt*. *Infāq* has been translated as the inclination to give rather than to take. This inclination is consistently fostered and inculcated throughout the Qur'ān. The periodic fixed share of wealth which is mandatory is minimal, and as such constitutes the base-line of *infāq*. Whatever the Muslim spends of his own free will beyond the fixed share becomes a *ṣadaqa,* literally 'an act of truth'. It attests to his devotion to his pledge in the *shahāda* and as such it is credited to an open account as a Beautiful Loan, or a Loan of Goodness *(qarḍ ḥasan)* which God, in His Munificence recompenses in His own true measure on the Day of Judgement (2: 245 and 5: 11). To make this Munificent Bargain even more appealing, to cultivate a worldly altruism to its utmost, and to urge the Muslim to give of the best he can afford, whatever he spends in the way of the needy, or in promoting the Good, it is qualified as *iḥsān* (an act of excellence; a striving to excel and perfect what you do). This is why the Divine Act of Reciprocity, in rewarding the giving disposition is promised to be in kind. The logic of this appeal is irrefutable: Can the Reward of *iḥsān* be anything other than *iḥsān*! (55: 60).

In times when so much social strife and ideological controversy in our societies is rooted in the attitude to material wealth and in the repercussions of this attitude, the pillar of *żakāt* and the ethos that surrounds it provide a salutary corrective. They remain a powerful and effective guide to individual conduct and to social action and organization.

Fasting: *Ṣiyām* (sing. *Ṣawm*)

In the pursuit of the Pillars of the Faith one is ascending a spheric spiral. What began with a Profession is steadily crystallizing into a progressive intensification of an act that encompasses nothing less than the whole of our being. At the beginning was the Uttered Word, an avowed pledge of the mortal self to a Creed, and the unfolding sequence is the committed Deed. After all we should remember that '*īmān* is that which rests in the heart and is confirmed by the deed/the conduct'. In *ṣalāt* and *zakāt* this confirmation was observable for all to see and to pursue. It is the *niyya* however, the purity of intention, that transforms a ritual into an act of devotion and that in this way saves it from waning into an empty gesture, i.e. it saves it from formalism. Yet how can one ascertain that one's intentions *are* pure?

So, how can one ascertain that in complying with the commands of God one is doing so out of pure devotion, not motivated by a desire for worldly fame and glory, or by the quest of prestige within the community? How can one avoid perverting these actions into a means for assuming a detestable self-righteousness – an ingredient in the smug 'holier than thou' attitude on the individual level and beyond that, a means of subverting religion to selfish purposes, a form of playing politics? Conversely, how can one assure that one's devotions are not just a matter of habit, when it is not expediency? After all, a habit degenerates into mindless usage or into 'custom' that ultimately preserves the form and divests itself of any meaning. In short, how can rituals be saved from their own momentum that robs them of their essence and hardens them into outer forms that strangle the living Faith. More often, they come to be celebrated/sanctified as the ways of the fathers by the sons – an attitude severely censured by the Qur'ān (2: 170, 5: 104, 31: 21). The answer to these questions is to be sought and found in the function of the 'fourth pillar' of *ṣiyām,* or the Fast as it is prescribed in Islam.

Fasting is the one devotion where the devotee can have no direct or obvious worldly dividend. In fasting he is denying himself, in total self-negation. There is no visibility about his state, his sole Witness is God. According to Tradition, Allah (SWT) says: 'All the devotions of the Son of Adam are for himself except Fasting which is done for Me, and it is I Who reward for it.' Indeed, of all the tests of the *shahāda,* it is the toughest and most exacting of its training grounds. Here, unlike the tangible and the material, which is the domain of *zakāt,* the domain in this instance is the most elusive of agents in the human being, namely the *nafs*. This is the inner Self, or the heart, which is the seat of the human intent and the source of the purity of the *dīn*. While all the Pillars of the Faith are a test of Deed by Intent, in Fasting we find ourselves involved in squaring the root of Intent by purging the corrosive sediments of the heart (passions and worldly desires).

Fasting goes beyond regulating the diet by refraining from all food and drink between dawn and sunset for the duration of its lunar month to prescribing a code of behaviour entailing self-restraint in some directions and self-exertion in others. Here, the Fast becomes an act of restraining and conditioning the senses in an exercise aimed at expanding the 'respiratory tracts' of the inner self. In *zakāt,* the object of sanctification/purification was the material possessions of the individual and the community, the object in *ṣiyām* is the *nafs* (the soul). And just as *zakāt* is a means of assuring growth and prosperity, so too is *ṣiyām* a means of growth and reinforcement of that Intangible which issues forth from the heart, namely, the Intent, the Will, the Resolve. More than an act of self-denial for the sake of God, *ṣiyām* is perceived by the devotee as an act of self-discipline willingly undertaken in the Way of God, i.e. as prescribed by Him, in fulfilment of His Command and in the quest of His Pleasure.

The way in which the Fast is prescribed ensures that it is primarily an act of restraint, control and reorganization, rather than simply deprivation. The timing of the Fast, its association with the *tanzīl,* the Revelation of the Qur'ān, gives the direction in which this reorganization and restructuring of the Muslim's lifestyle during this period should take. In this way the act of purifying the *nafs* and nourishing it, or maintaining its sound growth and development are simultaneously ensured so as to secure the substance of devotion/*'ibāda* in an affirmative and dynamic disposition. The same logic underlying the *shahāda* avails itself with equal vigour and impact in *ṣiyām*. In *shahāda* there is a basic profession of intent that enjoins absolute submission and total commitment in one and the same act, and the Creedal formula in which this intention is expressed is itself based on a total negation of all deities, thus paving the way for the exclusive and all-conclusive affirmation of the One True God – Allah (SWT). So it is in *ṣiyām*.

The Muslim is engaged in an act of cleaning out his innermost self from all the dross and accretions that contaminate it, so as to prepare the 'container' for the substance, rather, the sustenance and the inspiration it is about to receive. In this way the month of the Fast, Ramaḍān, becomes a month of intensified devotion when attention to the other Pillars too is stimulated. In fact, everything in the span of the Muslim's being is brought into closer focus and is directed together with a renewed dedication of the Community to the Source of its Faith and Strength in the Qur'ān. Visibly, the cycle of worldly preoccupations slows down and the re-arranged priorities of the Muslim compel him to pause for a period to take cognizance of the root and source of this Faith and identity. Otherwise, he is likely to fall into forgetfulness and neglect, or he will continue to take such basic questions so much for granted that they will cease to have any effective meaning for his life.

The practice of *i'tikāf* (retreat) symbolizes this state of intensified devotion. Towards the end of the month, in the last ten days, some devotees, following the example of the Prophet (peace be upon him), go into a state of retreat. Here the Muslim cuts himself off from all worldly contacts and preoccupations and dedicates himself exclusively to God, in a self-proclaimed state of devotional vigilance which involves a pulsating rhythm of withholding and upholding, abstaining and maintaining: a cycle of *ṣiyām* and *qiyām* (performing *ṣalāt* and reciting and studying the Qur'ān). His whole life for that short period of the year becomes a didactic theophany from his Creator: an intensification of the experience of His Imminence and all-encompassing Presence and a profound awareness of the bond and Pledge that binds the devotee to his Lord and Creator. Clearly, this critical self-awareness with the critical self-examination it entails, which is magnified here in the practice of *i'tikāf,* is a process experience in the Community at large in varying degrees and phases throughout this month. Little wonder, for it is one of the major purposes of this Pillar.

Yet for all its focus on the inner and the intangible in the individual believer, this Pillar, perhaps even more so than the others, has its repercussions on the 'outer' and the communal dimension of the Faith. Paradoxically, the deed of the Faith that is the least visible becomes the occasion for the public and manifest affirmation of the unity and identity of the *Umma,* the Community of Islam, beyond local neighbourhood and across political boundaries as the lifestyle of the fellowship of devotees is ostensibly transformed into a concordance of affinities. At no other time perhaps, are the outward ways and modes that bind the Community more directly related to their inner anchors than they are here during the month of Ramaḍān. For the individual Muslim, the Fast remains ultimately a matter of conscience; spiritually, he may or may not have fulfilled its purpose of enhancing his own God-consciousness/*taqwā.* For the Community as a whole though, the practice which impinges directly on a rigorous month-long lifestyle provides a periodic annual confirmation of its common identity. It also constitutes the occasion for renewing its spiritual affinities.

The Pilgrimage to Makka: *Ḥajj*

Where the *shahāda* was an act of bearing witness to the Unseen and of taking in this Invisible Presence a life-binding Pledge to bow to the Will and Command of Allah (SWT), the Pilgrimage, or *Ḥajj* is the culmination of an act of Faith. It is the materialization of the Witness and the Pledge. Similarly, *ṣalāt, zakāt* and *ṣiyām* were shown to be devotions mutually supportive and mutually reinforcing in inculcating the sense of *taqwā,* which is the central ethos of the Faith. In the *ḥajj,* the fifth pillar of the faith, this over-arching awareness of God is intensified to the exclusion of everything else.

Likewise, where the other Pillars, each in itself and all together, serve to instil that pervasive sense of community at the same time that they are forming and imparting the traits of that Community, so here in the *ḥajj* the impact of this community is fully realized. More than the summation and the materialization of the Faith and the Community, in the *ḥajj* temporality itself is yet another unseen as he is brought face to face with the *mashhad* (literally, the Witnessed Spectacle). The belief in the Hereafter which entails the belief in the raising from the dead and a Day of Judgement, is an article of the Muslim's Faith. In Qur'ānic Arabic, several terms are used to qualify this Day, the *Yawm al-dīn* (the Day of the Religion) as the Day of the Reckoning, of the Decision, of the Resurrection, or simply as The Hour. It is in the *ḥajj,* on the Plain of 'Arafāt, at the foot of *Jabal al-Raḥma* that the Muslim comes to have a foretaste and a glimpse of this awesome and awe-inspiring Spectacle. 'Arafāt literally connotes 'the making of acquaintance with', the 'meeting' and the 'knowing'; *Jabal al-Raḥma* can be translated as the Mount of Mercy. It is not surprising that *Sūra al-Ḥajj* in the Qur'ān begins with a sonorous reminder of The Hour.

The Qur'ān is resonant with vivid accounts of *yawm al-dīn*. It appeals to it as the Day of the Ultimate Reckoning 'when the witnesses will stand forth' – as Absolute Justice is meted out down to an 'atom's weight', and where Judgement is irrevocable (40: 51, 52; 99: 7–8). The very inculcation of God-consciousness in the believer with the injunction to heed his Creator and Judge in all his deeds, is geared to his notion of personal accountability. Here in the *ḥajj,* the multitudes wake to find themselves gathered, nay, packed in that parched plain where they spend the day until sundown under an open sky in the scorching heat. With the meagre provisions, against a background of transience and emptiness, only accentuated by the clusters of white pitched tents at the foot of the Mount, the pilgrims literally 'stand' in the presence of their Lord and Judge. It is in a state of naked isolation, exposed and alone, shorn of all but His Mercy, that they wait, subdued and extinguished, in the grip of a momentous tension and intensity. Fraught and overwhelmed, with a mixture of overpowering and conflicting emotions combining fear and anticipation, anxiety and hope, extenuation and elation – all of which he experiences in rapid succession, or at one and the same time, in a compressed moment that spans and distils a lifetime and seems to stretch out into an eternity – the pilgrim is forged in an experience beyond measure that leaves its indelible impact on his psyche for the rest of his life. In fact, the *ḥajj* is an experience that cuts deep into the individual psyche and leaves its permanent marks on the Community as a whole.

In fact, there is a historical dimension which underlies much of the collective consciousness of the Community and that owes so much to the *ḥajj*. It is at the roots of much that brings together the 'Peoples of Islam' from Indonesia and Central Asia to Morocco and West Africa. But this provides a theme in itself for another presentation.

The *ḥajj* provides an excellent point at which we can recapitulate the Pillars of the Faith in a brief survey of five of the rites prescribed for the pilgrim in Islam. There are the *ṭawāf,* the circumambulation of the Ka'ba, the *sa'ī,* the trekking back and forth between the hills of Ṣafā and Marwa; the *wuqūf* or the Standing at 'Arafāt; the *uḍḥīya* or the ritual sacrifice; and the *jamarāt* or the stoning of the Devil. It may be recalled that all these rites take place in Makka and its precincts, within a ten to twenty mile radius, and that at the heart of Makka is the Ka'ba. These rites taken together and each in itself are integral to the Faith and constitute the embodiment and condensation of its central tenets. They indicate the thrust of its belief-system and its way of life.

(1) *Tawḥīd* is the cornerstone of the *shahāda* and the bedrock of the Faith. As we have seen, it is the absolute affirmation of the Oneness of God in all its consequences foremost of which are the unity of Religion, the unity of Revelation and the unity of the mission and tradition of prophethood. *Tawḥīd* also recalls the basic unity of mankind, as it hails from a single common stock, and a Single Source unto which all are returned. This ultimate unity further embraces life itself whether it is conceived spatially or temporally along the continuum of relativity – (Past-Present-Future) – a continuum that ultimately transcends history. The single most powerful and most visible expression of this message is to be experienced in the orbiting of the Ka'ba in *ṭawāf*.

(2) Islam gives a sacred status to the ideal of purity *(ikhlāṣ)* as a condition and a derivative of *tawḥīd*. It exemplifies the Pure Religion and ordains the Pure Devotion, i.e. the religion and devotion which are not tainted with any form of human accretion, vanity or associationism *(shirk)*. If devoted and unreserved submission to the Will of God is one side of the coin, then peace,

serenity and security is the other side. The *ḥajj* carries with it these meanings in its model and in its inception. Abraham (Ibrāhīm) and his son Ismā'īl (upon whom be peace) embody the historical archetype of the Muslim in this sense and it is in their footsteps that the pilgrims follow. Moreover, it is to be recalled that the pilgrim starts his Sacred Journey by entering into a state of *iḥrām*. This may be translated as a state of abstinence and sanctification which is outwardly visible in a code of dress and conduct and which symbolizes a fundamental orientation towards a state of peace that envelops the totality of Creation.[2]

(3) Any notions about worship/devotion suggesting a restful retreat or a pause on the margins of an active life are clearly misplaced. In Islam *'ibāda* may originate passively, but it calls for nothing short of a totally active and dynamic affirmation of being that spans the life of the devotee in all its walks. This entails endless resources of energy matched to a tireless resolve to expend. All the rites of *ḥajj* are geared to this concept of active worship. In themselves, they involve a considerable self-exertion and strain, upon the psyche and the physical, and at the same time they condition the Will and renew its energy sources.

(4) Submission to the Will of the Creator recalls an act of Covenant: a binding pledge that commits the Muslim throughout his life unto death. The rites in the *ḥajj* crystallize this Pledge and bring it to the fore of his consciousness from the moment he sets foot in the Holy Sanctuary and faces the door of the Ka'ba before starting *ṭawāf*. This door is called *bāb al-multazim* which literally means the gate of one who takes the pledge. It is there that the Muslim renews his *shahāda* and confirms his Oath. Its corollary is an assertion of his personal responsibility. The sequel to this stance is in the *wuqūf* where the pilgrim comes to know in all certainty that accounts will be definitively settled on the Last Day, a Day of which there is no doubt.

(5) Striving to keep his Covenant with God, a Muslim is reminded of the noble task or Calling for which humans were created and commissioned to a set term on this earth.[3] He is equally reminded of the obstacles and distractions to its fulfilment. He must be made wary of them and must be adequately prepared morally and physically to resist and to overcome them.

CHAPTER 3

The Ka'ba: Its Symbolism and Related Rites

Prelude

Introducing Islam from within means explaining the main doctrines of the Faith as a Muslim understands them. It also means going beyond the forms which an outsider may observe when he sees a Muslim practise his Faith to ask about the possible meaning these practices may have for devotees. Tawḥīd *highlighted the central doctrine, belief and article of Faith in Islam. The Pillars showed how the basic duties are related to one another and to that doctrine. Our sequel here is to move from what the Muslim believes in and how he acts, to the values that he cherishes and the things that he values. These 'things' are tokens of the Faith and they may include such items as a prayer-mat, a rosary, a Qur'ān-stand, a compass to orient in prayer, a veil kept pure and clean, an incense-burner, an emblem or design, etc. Such items he does not cherish for themselves, but for what they represent. They carry a symbolic value, which the Muslim associates with his beliefs, affections, and practices. Foremost of these 'objects' to the Muslim is the 'noble sanctuary' for which the Ka'ba, at first instance, stands. There is nothing particularly mystical or mysterious about the 'holiest of holies' in Islam. The Ka'ba is held dear because in the simple and direct language of the Qur'ān: This was the first House built on earth to consecrate the worship of the One God. It is moreover, a place of assembly, a refuge and security for all humans. The site was as old as Adam and Eve, the first human beings to worship the One True God. God directed Abraham to this site where he laid the foundations for the House that stands there to this day. What is the history of that venerable site? More important, how is that history related to the history of the Pure Religion?*

In Islam we learn to appreciate the meaning of integrality: of how everything comes to fall into place to give meaning to and contribute to an edifice or structure that is itself whole. The cornerstone of this edifice as we learned was tawḥīd *(the affirmation of the absolute Oneness of God and its implications for the world-view and way of life that accompany such an act). The basic duties uphold* tawḥīd. *The Ka'ba itself embodies and reinforces* tawḥīd. *We also learned that Islam is Faith and Community as well as creed and history. How does the Ka'ba convey and affirm these elements?*

Such are the questions to ask as we look searchingly and critically into the exposition that follows.

The symbolism evoked by the Ka'ba and by the traditions associated with it is a subject that can fill volumes. As Islam is a religion of relatively few symbols however due to the openness, rationality and practicality of the Faith, the purpose of this limited presentation is to illustrate how, where symbols do occur the very nature of this symbolism conforms with and confirms the nature of the Faith. Central and foremost among the symbols in Islam is beyond doubt the Ka'ba itself, with the rituals associated with it. To anyone unfamiliar with the tenacity and purity of the core Islamic concept of *tawḥīd,* the veneration in which the Ka'ba with its enigmatic black stone is held, may be the source of some mystery and confusion. Some may, even out of sheer ignorance rather than malicious intent, attribute such veneration to vestiges of paganism. To the Muslim however, the Ka'ba is no more than what God calls it in the Qur'ān: *al-bait al-ḥarām* (the Sacred House) and *baitullāh* (the House of God). To the extent that the Muslim's world and life revolve around an exclusive and pure devotion to the One True God, the Sanctuary that God has appointed for man as a tangible point in space and time to assemble in and to 'visit', comes to partake of the sanctity and devotion directed to its Master. It is this *association* with its historical and ritual or symbolic dimensions that has made the Ka'ba a unique focus for the intense devotions of the Faithful down the centuries. It is thus important to categorically dispel any kind of unfounded doubts in this regard by exploring the historical and ritual significance of the Ka'ba to the millions of Muslims who flock there to visit or to perform the *ḥajj* – and to the countless others whose dream it is to perform but a few *rak'as* (ritual prayers) in its sanctuary. Indeed, to anyone familiar with the site the pilgrim must indeed be highly motivated by a consuming Faith and a pure devotion to want to make the journey in the first place. For there is little by way of worldly enjoyment to be found there in the scorched and barren desert. The Seeker is primarily impelled in his arduous journey by the yearning for an experience that transcends the joys and pleasures associated with this world.

The Ka'ba is that simple cube stone building situated in the womb of the city of Makka, essentially in a crater surrounded by rocky hills in a barren valley. Historically, it is at the origins of the growth of the city which on its account retained a tradition of sacredness long antedating and anticipating the mission of God's Last Messenger (peace be upon him) who was born there. The Ka'ba is at the centre of other sites associated with that sanctification of what in the Qur'ān is called *umm al-qurā* (the Mother of Cities). The others are found in the two little hills, a few hundred yards from the Ka'ba itself, and most important of all, the Well of Zamzam – that miraculous source of sweet underground water that originally gushed forth under the feet of a baby boy at a remote point in time and which has ever since continued to flow and quench the thirst of many a pilgrim. It was this water that made possible any life or settlement in what was otherwise a forsaken spot in the Arabian wasteland. Today, and ever since the advent of historical Islam, these four sites are enclosed in what is known as the Noble Sanctuary, and are integral to the rites of the *ḥajj*.

According to the Qur'ān, the Ka'ba is the first House built in consecration to the worship of the One True God. Its foundations were laid by Abraham and his son Ismā'īl at God's Command and so were the rites of worship that were instituted in it (3: 96–7; 2: 125, 128; 22: 26). With time, and especially in the half millennium before the advent of the Prophet (peace be upon him) the ever-surviving heritage of a pure monotheism from the Abrahamic origins of the Faith were buried under a welter of human accretion and folly that finally degenerated during a period of almost global chaos into a rampant paganism. Yet despite its contamination, the site never lost its aura or sacredness as the pre-Islamic tradition of Arabia amply attests. This history further points to another repository of the Abrahamic legacy of the Pure Religion in a 'heretic' sect that held aloof from the ways and customs of their people and nurtured a vague memory and innate conviction of the One True God. These were known as the *ḥanīfs*. The other residue of the Abrahamic tradition associated with Makka was a curious and unlikely Code – given the feuding and war-ridden nature of pagan Arabia. It was found in a cult of peace and asylum related to the Sanctuary and certain rites associated with it.

Thus, from time immemorial, from the inception of the channel of communication and guidance between heaven and earth, the True Religion *(al-dīn al-qayyim),* or 'generic Islam' was identified at its root as 'the act of submission to the One God'. Integral to this act and flowing from it was 'the Way of Peace': its pursuit and its experience. By the time polytheism and idolatry had submerged the 'Mother of Cities' and its surroundings, all that remained of the Pure Faith were its vestiges in a symbol and a tradition. The mission of the Prophet Muḥammad (peace be upon him) was the fulfilment of Revelation, of the Message of Guidance, not its beginning. It came to restore faith to its original purity. Abraham was the seed, the progenitor, of many nations and at the root of a chain of Prophets and Messengers sent to those nations. Part of the mission of restoring the Pure Religion was to mend the rifts that had grown and to rally those nations to a unity founded on the Pure Faith. In the Qur'ān the truth of that which had gone before is confirmed and the controversies and the ambiguities into which the successors of the earlier Messengers and the guardians of the message had lapsed were now resolved. In this sense, the Qur'ān is variously referred to and described as the *Clarification, al-bayān,* and as the conclusive standard, or the *Criterion, al-furqān,* brought down as the Seal of all Prophethood and Revelation.

In this sense too the fundamental message of Islam was not new. What was new was the form this Message took, its dimensions and its scale. Henceforth, the message of God was to be preserved in a Book, immune to the ravages of time and the folly of man, but open and accessible to all who sincerely sought

Guidance. The repository of the Faith was in the Community at large, and the human being, whoever he might be and wheresoever, was credited with an inherent dignity and vested with a sacred mission in the *khilāfa*.[1] Henceforth, no group of human beings could stand above others nor claim the privilege of a special knowledge or a special mission not open to others. Nor could any group or any individual come between the human being and his Creator, the worshipper and the Worshipped. With the principles of a fundamental equality and justice rooted in a pious conscience, and with the elements of a 'nomocracy' embedded in a Constitution open to everyone, all clergies and theocracies would become obsolete, as there would be neither a class to arrogate power and corrupt it, nor a system to sanctify abuse and maintain it. These are the chief implications of the new form the Last Guidance took. They underline the liberating essence of its core concept and foundation, *tawḥīd.*

It is this liberating essence which constituted in the past as it does today the revolutionary component and the regenerative momentum of the Faith. These elements continue to retain their force and relevance thanks to the uncontaminated purity of its sources and its core tenets in a context where change is only accentuated by certain perennial dimensions in the human condition. So much for the significance of the Ka'ba in the historical context of the Revealed Guidance of *tanzīl*. To review some aspects of its enduring symbolism the following points should be emphasized.

1. The Ka'ba remains symbolic of an essence: the idea of the Prime and the Core. It is the first House on earth built to consecrate the One True God and it has remained ever since at the centre of a continuous tradition of human worship and devotion. More particularly it is symbolic of the integrating and the unifying power of monotheism in human life. These ideas are themselves integral to the concept of Islam as the Religion of pure Monotheism *(dīn al-tawḥīd)*. It celebrates and upholds the unity of all true religion by affirming its Prime Source. Its worldview takes the One True God Allah (SWT) as the focus and the integrating core for an entire belief-system that relates and coheres round that Core.

2. The idea of the Prime and the Core lends itself to interpretation at different levels which all serve to reinforce and confirm the basic concepts of Islam as the Religion of Pure Monotheism, and hence as the One True Religion for all men and for all time. The historic association with the Abrahamic Tradition illustrates the point. Abraham is upheld in the Qur'ān, not for his ancestry of the Arabs but for being the model and the archetype of the Muslim, pure and true in his total self-surrender to the One and Only God and no other. Where progeny is an issue, it is to demonstrate that Abraham is at the source and start of a lineage of Prophets and a cycle of Revealed Guidance from the Creator to the human world. Hence, Abraham, as the 'Father of the Prophets' was neither Jew nor Christian for he came before the Revealed Scripture to either, and the path he blazed which all the subsequent Messengers followed: the path of submission to the One True God Alone and devotion to His Command: i.e. 'Islam'. In its association with the Abrahamic Tradition and its commemoration of it, the Ka'ba becomes symbolic of the unity of all True Religion, celebrates the brotherhood of all Prophets and the essential unity of their message, and thus establishes the Brotherhood of the Faithful down the ages/generations.

3. The Ka'ba is not just associated with the beginnings of the Pure Faith and of religion as it is consecrated in its Abrahamic origins. But it has since confirmed and consecrated its summation in the pristine purity of its faith as it crystallized and came to be preserved in the One True Religion. This was the purpose and the achievement of the mission of the last Prophet and Servant-Messenger of God. Muḥammad (peace be upon him) born in Makka in 570 A.C. came in the full lineage and tradition of the Abrahamic stock, to put an end to one cycle of Divine Guidance and to initiate another that was to carry humanity through to its 'Appointed Hour'. As the Seal of the Prophets he came to close the cycle of prophethood by confirming their mission and purifying it of the accretions of time, and, by summing it up and underlining its central message. This message is one and the same and it retains its validity for all nations and for all time. Such was the homage and the tribute paid in the mission of the last of God's Messengers to the Abrahamic heritage which had in the space of time between the

beginning and the end, become either totally submerged beneath a welter of accretions, or distorted beyond bounds.

The fate of the Ka'ba demonstrated the first instance that religion there had, before the coming of the Prophet, degenerated into a blatant idolatry and the sanctuary of Makka, as the cradle of monotheism in all its purity, could no longer be recognized as such. Elsewhere, the Abrahamic origins had been periodically renewed and rectified with the sequence of Messengers and Prophets who were sent to their people. They remained however subject to such distortion and confusion until, by the time of the rise of Muḥammad (peace be upon him), the Message of Peace and Truth had itself become a source of much discord and strife among its adherents. Such discord was contradictory to the purpose of True Religion, which is to unite, not to divide, to integrate not to separate, and to enlighten and make crystal clear, not to dim and to render ambiguous or steeped in mystery.

The mission of the Last Messenger was thus fore-ordained. It was literally to clear up the debris that had grown round the Holy Sanctuary and to communicate the pure Faith to a people there who had until then received no Prophet of their own, nor any Book. At the same time this Message was addressed to the People of the Book, the Jews and the Christians, in order to resolve the points of dispute among them (including such topical issues as the nature of Christ), and to recall them to the essence of the Abrahamic monotheistic tradition. It invited them to enter into the Pact of Peace by accepting Islam (See the *āya* where Islam and Peace are used interchangeably, by contracting I-S-L-A-M to its root *S-L-M*) (2: 208). In doing so it was inviting them to renew and confirm that perennial Tradition embodied and consecrated in the Ka'ba.

4. The mission of the Last Messenger was to inaugurate an era in which Divine Guidance was to assume a new form. Its address was openly universal, its scope wider and more comprehensive, and its injunctions were spelled out in detail. In the final stage of Guidance or *tanzīl,* Prophets sent to their own people and at specific junctures with particular signs would cease to be the mediators between Heaven and Earth. Henceforth, parochialism and guardianship would give way to an era of universalism and globalism where humanity would come of age and come to

appreciate its affinities and the common goals which united it more than the differences which divided it. In this coming of age, the responsibility for man's fate and moral well-being would come to rest squarely on his own free choice and on a willing initiative to respond to his Creator. Reason would constitute the device; and the Sign to which one was now left the choice to respond to was the Recorded Revelation of the last transmitted Divine Guidance. Historically preserved in its original form, word for word, and communicated down the ages in the very sequence and order prescribed for it by the 'Faithful and True', the Qur'ān was in a position to challenge and beacon all who would care to reflect.[2]

Muḥammad (peace be upon him), the last of the Prophets and Apostles of God, was confirmed in his prophetic mission *vis-à-vis* those who had preceded him among the Prophets, and in his humanity *(bashariyya)* he was confirmed *vis-à-vis* a posterity that would be invited to join the Community he had founded and left behind. For this Community, or *Umma,* he would continue to provide the human model and example in a Tradition embodying the precepts of the Faith and constituting a historical chart of the Way.[3] Henceforth too, the spiritual renewal and regeneration of the human being would become his own responsibility as the historical mechanism would be reversed to the benefit of an independent and mature humanity. In the earlier cycle of Divine Guidance, renewal and regeneration had been contingent on the advent of emissaries/Prophets. In the latter cycle, they would become contingent on the emergence of social movements that would come to turn for their renewed inspiration and commitment, to the now constantly preserved Source of Guidance – in the Qur'ān.

The Ka'ba thus becomes symbolic not only of the origins of the One True Religion, but a living testimony to its vigour and its continued appeal to an expanding circle of a global humanity. As the multitudes continue to be drawn to a sanctuary cradled in the womb of an arid valley in the barren sands of Arabia, flocking in from all corners of the world, the triumph of the principle of Universalism converges with an affirmation of the principle of Pure Monotheism.

5. The Ka'ba is symbolic of an orientation as well as a principle. If the principle is the Absolute and Uncompromising Unity of God, the One and Only God, Who takes no partners unto Himself and Who begets not nor is He begotten, and to whom nothing and nobody can be compared – which is what 'pure monotheism' is about – the Orientation refers to the response called forth by man to God. If God is One and humanity is one, and if the Religion that binds that humanity to God is One, then it follows that the greatest integrative force for men is to be found in that One Religion, and that the symbol of this cohesive bond is manifest in the direction the believers face when they set out to perform their devotions. This idea of a common orientation and a common goal is institutionalized through the prototype of the Original house consecrated to the One True God, in every Mosque by its *miḥrāb* – or niche – an architectural device pointing in the direction of the Ka'ba. Wherever a Muslim stands to pray, and bow and prostrate himself in devotion to the One True God, to Allah, he sets his face towards the *qibla* – in the direction of the Ka'ba; in doing so he is reminded of the source of identity and of the common purpose and goal which binds him to his Community in Faith. Thus, the Ka'ba which is historically the symbol of the Unity of Religion and the consecration of the Unity and the Oneness of the Only True God, comes to symbolize and consecrate the Unity, Equality and brotherhood of those who bow themselves in willing submission to Him Alone and are committed to the Guidance and the Way He has chosen for them.

6. Inasmuch as the Ka'ba is symbolic of primal origins and is rooted in a timeless antiquity, that same stone cube in its stark simplicity also stands as a monument to a permanence and a constancy in the tidal fluctuations of a mortal humanity. But, more important perhaps than the idea of roots and continuity is the symbolism of renewal and a capacity for renewability with which it is associated. Indeed, the impact of the *ḥajj* on the Community in Islam has been likened to the blood circulation in the body – with its perennial infusion and renewal of the Faith throughout the worldwide Community of Islam. More specific is the pledge which every Muslim makes upon entering the precincts of the Holy Sanctuary, as he approaches the Ka'ba. As

he faces its door, and before setting off on the first round of the *ṭawāf* (circumambulation), he stands as in an act of Covenant to profess the two testimonies of the Faith (the *shahāda*) and to renew his pledge of commitment. In this situation, the profession which the Muslim will have uttered hundreds of times over in his daily prayers now takes on new dimensions that overawe the believer – so that once experienced, the *shahāda* is not likely to be seen in the same way again. As the Muslim stands in solemn humility at this station he identifies with a whole series of similar stations and situations in which the *bai'a* (oath of allegiance) was taken, whether in the course of the early history of Islam during the lifetime of the Prophet (peace be upon him) or whether within the tradition of generic Islam, which stems from the invocation and the pledge by Abraham and his son Ismā'īl as they lay the foundations of the Ka'ba.

In fact, it is in the very words recorded in the Qur'ān for these occasions that the pilgrim finds himself rehearsing and expressing the intensity of the moment as he reconsecrates himself anew. It is this act that gives its name to the door of the Ka'ba, which is known as *Bāb al-Multazim*: literally, the gate or the door of the one who takes the oath, or makes the pledge and the commitment. Indeed, every detail, every ritual in the *ḥajj* and in the lesser pilgrimage (the *'umra*) has a meaning that goes beyond the form and which combines the historical and the symbolical dimensions in a dramatic concordance that imparts its momentum on the psyche and the spirituality of the believer. Nowhere is this comment more true than with the rituals that are prescribed for the Ka'ba and its precincts.

7. The *Bāb al-Multazim* with its symbolic connotation constitutes a 'fringe detail' if we were to compare it with another of the ritual ordinances which prefaces or inaugurates the sequence of rites that follow and make up the Pillars of the *ḥajj*. This opening act is so crucial and integral a part of the whole that it is the condition for the acceptance or the validity of all that follows. It is known as the *iḥrām* or the state of sanctification and abstinence which pilgrims enter into when they go on *ḥajj*. Its visible signs are demonstrable in a code of dress and behaviour. It parallels the ritual ablutions and the proclamation of *niyya,* or intent, which precedes the performance of prayers – and it possibly

provides us with the most dramatic illustration of the centrality of an *ethic of intention* to the Muslim conscience. For this is the ethic which underlies all the devotions in Islam.[4] If we recall that the span of devotion is that of life itself and that it is the intent that assures the concordance between the inner and the outer dimensions of life for the individual and for the community alike, then we can realize the meaning of the sanctity embodied in the Sanctuary at Makka. Nurtured in this intimate concordance, Islam as Peace, peace between self/Creator, self/self, and self/world is experienced at its ultimate in this sanctity-imbued state of *iḥrām* in the Ka'ba.

The True Religion is a religion of dynamic and integrated balance which welds together the moral and the social fabric into an intrinsic whole. As we have seen earlier, the prescribed devotions, as in the Pillars of the Faith, constitute the testing and training ground where the welding and forging of this fabric takes place. It is in this context too that *iḥrām* which inaugurates the cycle of rites here is generally seen. At a deeper level of inter-relating the Pillars and establishing parallels and concordances – which again is another feature of the Islamic ethos – *iḥrām* is nothing less than the recapitulation and the embodiment of the Creedal Formula of the *shahāda* in all its fullness. Where the *Bāb al-Multazim* station was an act-in-all-consciousness conducive to an accentuated state of consciousness, here in *iḥrām* the compound act of divestment and of re-dedication which it involves is the symbolic re-enactment, or the literal living out of the meaning of *Lā ilāha illa-llāh*: the absolute affirmation of the One and Only God through a double negation.

Put in other terms, the one who goes into the state of *iḥrām* sees to it that all his worldly debts have been settled before he removes all worldly attire, washes his body and embalms it in fresh attire, and clear in mind and heart, re-dedicates himself to the Way of his Creator. This parallels the *shahāda* which in a way it re-enacts at another concrete level of experience. For *shahāda* as we may recall, is the exclusive and conclusive affirmation that is preceded by a total and absolute negation. In this sense, it is the quintessence of the purity of the Faith that is celebrated in the 'Pure Religion' as the heart of the believer is emptied out, purged of all its idols and vain allegiances, to make way for the exclusive and undivided allegiance to The One.

Here again, the Ka'ba is at the heart of this symbolism. This meaning was historically associated with the conquest of Makka, the eradication of paganism and the reconsecration of the Sanctuary to the True Religion. In pagan Arabia, the Ka'ba had been surrounded by scores of idols; tradition has it that there were 360 in all, one for each day of the lunar year. With the final triumph of Islam, in the eighth year of the *hijra*, the beloved Prophet (peace be upon him) rode around on his camel knocking down with his stick each one of them and reciting the *āya*: 'Truth has come, vanity is vanquished, truly all vanity is evanescent!' (see 17: 80, 81). The vibrations of this invocation still fill the air today as the dense human clusters compass the Ka'ba in *ṭawāf* in much the same way as they have continued to do so over the past fourteen centuries. Indeed, it is in this rite of *ṭawāf*, that the ultimate symbolism of the purity of Islamic monotheism, *tawḥīd*, is dramatically, repeatedly, vigorously, tirelessly and continuously upheld. It is the tuning in with a vibrant cosmic rhythm that embraces the entirety of Creation.[5]

It is little wonder that the Ka'ba continues to impart a fascination and an appeal unique to it. In the heart of every devotee who has experienced the Light of Truth and savoured of its beatitude, the Ka'ba occupies a very special place. On another more detached plane, the preservation of the Ka'ba, as a living symbol, down the generations to this day and age and its continuity as a haven of devotion, a shelter of refuge, and a site of grace *(baraka)* is, in itself, a sign – an *āya* – that invites serious reflection by all those who truly care to think.

Notes and References

1. The concepts of *khilāfa* and *amāna* were mentioned earlier, see Chapter 1. Also cf. Chapter 4.

2. Long before the Prophet received his Calling and Way, he was renowned among the people he grew up among for his truthfulness and honesty, so much so that he was named *al-ṣādiq al-amīn*. The arrangement of the Qur'ān in terms of the sequence of *sūras* and *āyas* was like the content itself a matter of prescription, not of an arbitrary tradition. See Appendix 3.

3. For the place of the *sunna*, or the Way of the Prophet (peace be upon him) in the historical consciousness of the Community, see Chapter 4.

4. For a brief description see Ghayth Nur (Lonnie) Kashif al-Hajji in *A Sacred Journey* (Washington 1985). Also see section on *ḥajj* in Chapter 2.

5. The visual presentation, in the sequence of Rites and Concordances conveys the point made here. Cf. in conjunction with reference to its twin rite, the *sa'ī*. See Chapter 1.

CHAPTER 4

*The Social and Political Implications of the Faith**

Prelude

Islam laid the foundations of civilizations among those who professed its faith and adopted its way. Today, these civilizations no longer exist. Instead, the Muslim peoples throughout Asia and Africa are emerging from the colonial experience and are striving to consolidate their independence and to develop their resources to meet their needs in a technological age. Islam the Faith, is still very much alive among the majority of Muslims today. In the struggle to recover their power and status among the nations of the world, the memory of the glory of bygone times inspires them. Further, Islam constitutes an important element of communal identity that the peoples of Islam share today – and seek to affirm. To understand how Muslims are reacting today in situations in which they perceive themselves to be disadvantaged, it is important to enquire into some of the social values and the collective ideals of Islam. How does the Muslim relate to society? How does he or she relate to history? Islam inculcates an 'activist ethos' – What does this mean? What is the nature of that ethos? These are some of the issues addressed in this chapter.

To underline the significance of these issues, and of how they concern a Western audience, our prelude may be extended to further observations. Islam has always been an important factor in conditioning social and public responses in the Muslim world. This is as true today as it was in the past. Yet modern scholars, as well as 'nationalists' and 'modernists' have tended to undermine,

---

*An edited reprint of this chapter has appeared in the *American Journal of Islamic Social Sciences*, Vol. 4, No. 1 (September 1987).

or to ignore, the relevance of the Islamic heritage to present-day Muslim societies. The events of the past decades, however, came to dislodge any illusions about the marginality of that heritage and faith to these societies. Moreover, the globe has considerably 'shrunk', and people all over the world are more likely than ever to be affected by events even in its remotest corner. The Middle East is not that 'remote corner', and the impact of Islam on the social and political developments of the times does not stop at the boundaries of the Muslim world (assuming that such boundaries still exist). Consequently, it is in everybody's interest to try to take the measure of this impact by an earnest attempt to understand the socio-political dimension of Islam. Why do the Muslims in different parts of the world react to the social and political events of our times in the way they do? What is it that makes such reactions in many ways similar, despite the distances and apparent barriers and divergences that separate these nations? This is all the more surprising in the absence of any efficient organizational format that operates transnationally (or nationally) to co-ordinate responses and mobilize Muslim public opinion. Surely, these peoples must share in a common matrix that conditions their responses and affects their motivation, understanding, ideals and aspirations. There must also be elements that are common to the circumstances in which they react.

The place for us to start is to explore the social and political implications of the Faith. By now we are familiar with the integrality of Islam; the fact that it cannot be compartmentalized. We have already seen aspects of that when examining the most general and basic concepts like 'īmān' *(faith),*' 'ibāda' *(worship) and the root idea of* 'khilāfa'. *Once these concepts are related to the historical setting where Muslims interact with events in evolving situations, then these social and political implications come to life; they become concrete. Our presentation here is highly restricted and selective. It broaches neither on the historical nor on the contemporary political setting. It simply highlights some of those social and collective ideals and values that are seen to underlie events. By doing so, it provides the reader with the elements of an individual sensibility and discernment, which he can then himself apply to understand the current developments that affect the Muslim world.*

These are some of the questions to look for in what follows in order to assimilate the contents:

- *What are the elements of the Muslim's historical consciousness?*
- *What is the name given to the Muslim Community? What is the source of solidarity within that Community?*
- *What are the central ideals of the Muslim Community?*
- *How does the Muslim understand 'Justice'? What is the nature of the Muslim's commitment to Justice?*
- *What does* 'Jihād' *mean? How is it related to other ideals and values to which the Muslim is committed?*
- *How does Islam inculcate an activist ethos on the one hand, and promote a positive social morality on the other?*
- *What is the Islamic concept of 'martyrdom'* – istishhād? *How does this concept compare with its counterpart in other cultures? How does it relate to other concepts?*
- *In what way may the* 'shahāda' *of the* 'mujāhid' *be related to the* 'shahāda' *of the confession of the faith?*

Islam is more than a Faith in the heart of every Muslim. It is also a source of identity. The fundamental rites and devotions constituting its 'pillars' were shown as simultaneously confirming the faith of the individual and affirming the bonds of the Community. It is this symbiosis of Faith and Community that over time gave rise to a Muslim historical consciousness. From it too stems the predilection for an active social and political involvement on the part of Muslims as groups and individuals. The elements of this consciousness emanate from an Islamic world-view and they have interacted in various situations and contexts to condition the responses of Muslims throughout history. To explore these elements it is essential to examine three basic concepts: *umma, 'adl, jihād* or respectively, Community, Justice and the Just Striving. All three concepts are embedded in the matrix of *tawḥīd* and are interwoven and integrally related to one another. In their context a Muslim group consciousness has been forged for over a millennium. As such, they justly provide the parameters for understanding Muslim history.

The Community in Islam is a purposeful entity composed of a group, or a *jamā'a* whose members, by virtue of a common faith, way of life and sense of destiny, have been forged in a common historical consciousness. They are thus endowed with an awareness of a common identity, allegiance and purpose. The roots of this awareness go back to the advent of the Prophet (peace be upon him), with the final and perfected Guidance calling people to the exclusive worship of the One God and showing them the Way to this devotion. The struggle in the path of conveying the Pure Faith to the hearts of men and women and of reforming their ways of thought and conduct in society accordingly constituted the formative groundwork for the emergent Community. To confirm this new Community in its identity and to break it into history so as to assume its role among other groups and collectivities, the last ten years of the life of the Prophet (peace be upon him) were given to this task. This was the period known in Muslim history as the Madina Era which also marks the beginning of the Muslim Calendar. During this period a comprehensive ethical legal framework for social organization was steadily established on the basis of Revealed Divine Guidance. Under the leadership and example of the Prophet (peace be upon him) the *umma* received its first practical lessons both in the principles of Justice and in persevering to uphold it. The ordeals and the triumphs of this core Community in encountering the challenges to its survival came to constitute the first milestones in the Muslim's historical consciousness. By the time the Revelation of the Qur'ān was completed, a full-fledged Community had also come of age with its distinctive character, institutions, common historical experiences, memories and aspirations. When the Prophet (peace be upon him) died, the worldly leadership of this Community passed to his successors who were chosen from among his earliest followers: and were also among the first members of the Community. This leadership was an acknowledgement that the Community was there to stay as a distinctive historical entity entrusted with a mission that it must continue to safeguard and uphold.

In fact, we can only appreciate the centrality of the Community in Islam and its worldly or temporal aspect by recalling the nature of Prophethood. Throughout the history of Revealed Religion, Prophets were the medium for the Divine Message.

Prophets were human beings who were chosen by God for delivering their people from their inequities by showing them the Right Way and putting before them their moral accountability. The cornerstone to this Reform was in teaching the Pure Faith *(Tawḥīd)* and the values and beliefs associated with it and urging people to set up their lives and worldly pursuits accordingly. With the coming of Muḥammad (peace be upon him) the chain of prophethood came to an end – but *not* the Message of Guidance.[1] This message, or Mission, was now entrusted to a Community that embodied its teachings and upheld the moral social order based on this Guidance. The Community was not a Church with its ordained clergy, but it was the common believers themselves entrusted with the responsibility of organizing themselves and choosing their leadership from amongst themselves. As such they constituted an elect Community privileged in view of their adherence to *tawḥīd* and to its way of life. To the extent that it neglects its injunctions it forfeits its title to God's Favours and to His election. This chosen Community, the *umma,* is unique both in its membership and in its purpose. It is not composed of a specific race, caste or class but of whomever has chosen *tawḥīd* for his creed and has by virtue of his *shahāda* pledged his will in devotion to his Creator and Sustainer and bonded himself in brotherhood to his fellow devotees. This is the meaning of the statement that Islam is a source of identity. In it all other marks of distinction that imply a sense of exclusiveness or an ascribed privilege are dissolved in a brotherhood of the Faith. In one's new allegiance, one also gains a new vision and a sense of common purpose that are all anchored in *tawḥīd.*

Reinforced in its constitutive bond and common direction (*qibla* and *wajh* or *ittijah*)[2] the *umma* survives as a distinct and recognizable historical entity among other communities. Its place and impact in history are not contingent upon its organizational form although doubtless, as it has learned from its own history, much of this impact and effectiveness depend on its effective leadership and organization. In this respect too, it is not exempt from the laws that govern history and society. Historically, the *umma* has always been associated with its political expression in the 'State'. The latter however, has little in common with the sovereign territorial entity or the modern nation-state which is solely of European provenance. Sovereignty in the Islamic State belongs to God alone. The State itself exists only as the representative of the group or the Community; its agents are chosen from among the members of the Community simply as instruments of the collectivity, i.e. as executives for the *Jamāʿa* who are thereby charged with implementing the Just Order prescribed by the *sharīʿa.*[3] *Shūrā, ijtihād*[4] and consensus *(ijmāʿ)* are working values that underlie the spirit of implementing the *sharīʿa* and assure it its continued vitality and relevance in meeting the needs of the organized/corporate community. In this way, leadership and political power are instrumental for fully realizing the potential of the Community in Islam. In view of their origin, nature and purpose however, they result in a distinctive institution that historically has been known as the 'Caliphate' *(al-khilāfa).*

Originally, the term *khilāfa* was applied to denote the successor of the Prophet (peace be upon him) as one who is entrusted by the Community, or the *Jamāʿa,* to oversee its common direction and to regulate its worldly affairs in the light of the Recorded Guidance and the example of the Prophet (peace be upon him). The Caliphate, by extension, became the Institution upholding the Just Order exemplified in the *sharīʿa* and symbolizing the unity of direction of the *umma.* Hence, it significantly came to stand for the unity of the *umma* and the immutability of an Order of Justice historically associated with that *umma* as heir to a divine heritage and mission.

While the Caliphate as such remained synonymous with the Islamic State in the historical consciousness of the Community, Muslims came to experience various forms of government that fell short of the ideal and political power was frequently abused. But the restraining impact of the *sharīʿa* and the pervasiveness of a commonly held ethos binding rulers and ruled and integrated to the belief-system of the Community, were generally effective in setting limits to such abuse. The fact that the hub of personal and social/public life in the Community was regulated in accordance with the *sharīʿa* and subject to an autonomous jurisdiction or court system, mitigated the consequences of arbitrariness or abuse in the 'Executive'. Interestingly, there are other terms (like *mulk* and *sulṭān*, lit. dominion, kingship and power) which are used in the Muslim tradition of learning and inquiry to designate political power as a conceptually neutral term that refers to a universal historical and sociological phenomenon.[5] This is not the place to explore them. But the important thing to remember is that for the *Umma*/Muslim Community an Islamic Order, with which the connotation of *Khilāfa* remains associated, has never lapsed as a realizable ideal that should be sought and restituted. Its recovery, under whatever form or name, is seen as a token of the rehabilitation of the worldly affairs of the Community and as an affirmation of Justice in Society.

Meanwhile the Community expanded and came to include diverse peoples/races and tongues. Despite such growth and variety it did not disintegrate or lose its character. *Tawḥīd* welded the groups and individuals together, while their resulting observance of a common code of life structured this unity. Long after its first moment, the common consciousness of the Muslims as a group continued to be moulded by a long history during which time they continued to identify themselves with the original community built by the Prophet (peace be upon him). What consistently sustained this sense of identity was the spread and perpetuation of the instruments of socialization together with the pervasiveness of the ethical-social code. Both sets of institutions were firmly anchored in the original Islamic Sources: the Qur'ān and the *sunna* of the Prophet. They continued to feed and inspire a tradition of scholarship and a cultural heritage which became the 'commonwealth' for successive generations.

Political power too circulated among diverse elements in the Community. Dynasties of varying fortunes rose and fell and alliances were made and broken. As far as the members of the *umma* were concerned, the stage was unfolding within a common arena that was familiar as *Dār al-Islām,* the House of Islam. Its moments of glory as well as those of peril, when the Islamic heritage and Order were threatened by an outside invasion or local turmoil, came to be etched in the group consciousness regardless of geography or territorial location. They were added to those moments of the formative phase to enrich the collective memory of the *umma*. This sense of common destiny was the natural sequel to the bond of *tawḥīd* and the allegiance that flows from it as it is transferred from the level of the individual Muslim conscience to that of the group.

Ultimately however, while the *umma* maintains its distinctiveness, its state of health and its fate remain bound to the state of its members as individuals and groups. As we shall see below, the notion of personal responsibility in Islam as well as its scope are such as to render every Muslim accountable for the Whole. In effect the practical example of the first generation of Muslims set the tone in this respect. Its members were brought up in the school of the Prophet (peace be upon him) and they were trained in teachings and precepts that continue to inspire and cultivate an effective social conscience whenever they are seriously invoked. 'You are all, each and everyone of you, entrusted with a charge and you are all, each and everyone of you responsible for that charge.' In their solidarity, 'The believers are to one another like a solid edifice (reinforcing one another), each binding the part to the whole.' The material bond is complemented by a spirituality: 'The example of the believers in their love, compassion and concern for one another is in the likeness of a (live) body where each and every member in it is alerted to a state of feverish solicitude the moment one of its members is afflicted.' The moral fibre of this body must be unbreakable: 'Should my Umma ever fear to openly denounce the Unjust (and face up to it) then it is fated to extinction.' There is no room for indifference: 'The example of the one who commits a transgression and the one who is its victim may be compared to (the fate) of a group aboard a ship. Some were on the top and others were below. When those who were below – tiring of climbing on deck with their buckets to haul water – got an idea: it was to bore a hole in their cabins below and obtain their water without bothering their deck inmates. In this case, if those above left those below free to pursue their ways, then surely all would perish; whereas if they checked them, then they, along with all the others, would be saved.' In this kind of Community there is no escaping one's responsibility for oneself and for the whole to which one belongs. 'Every Muslim is outposted on a vigil to the Day of Judgement.'

If the above instances from the *Ḥadīth* of the Prophet (peace be upon him) are taken together with the injunctions of the Qur'ān in this respect, a characteristic Community Profile emerges. 'You are the best of Communities set forth for humankind, (because) you enjoin the Right and forbid the Wrong and you believe in God.' In the light of its responsibilities, the *umma* is expected to dispose of the means to enable it to measure up to its charge (22: 41). It is thus called upon to be an effective force in history capable of supporting the Good wherever it finds it and countering the currents of Corruption and Evil wherever they may be at work. 'And thus have We made of you an *Umma Wasaṭ*/a Median Community, so that you may be Witnesses upon humankind, and We have rendered the Prophet a Witness upon you.' The *Umma* is here described as a Median Community in view of its calling to mediate Justice among nations. By setting itself up as an example in the way of Justice and by weighing the balance of history in favour of Justice it is assigned an affirmative responsibility designated as an act of bearing witness over mankind.

The *umma* constitutes the collective or group frame of reference within which the historical consciousness of the Muslims has evolved. The other elements of this consciousness are conceivable within its parameters along a means-ends spectrum. Justice lies at the heart of a core of integrally related social values which together are embedded in the bedrock of *tawḥīd*. As an *umma* sound in its foundations, possessed of a clear vision of its purpose and calling, it is equally empowered with the means to live up to its divinely-set standards and to realize them in time. This authority draws on a reserve of inculcated values which orients Muslims to assuming their charge. Hence, at the means end of the spectrum, lies the duty of *jihād* as the crowning expression of that ethos of *infāq*.[6] The historical consciousness of the Community is thereby wedded to a social conscience which begins with the responsibility of the Muslim towards his family and neighbourhood and extends to encompass his fellowship in humanity at large. In this perspective, wherever the values that impinge on the freedom and dignity of the individual or the community are threatened, justice is itself seen to be at stake and the Muslim is duty bound to be in the forefront of their defence. Transferred to the collectivity it is this commitment to Justice that is equated to assuming the burden of 'bearing Witness unto nations' – as the *umma*'s profile illustrated. Where the Community falls short on its ideal whether through neglecting its standards or defuncting on the means, the ideal and the commitment will still continue on the personal or individual level and it will find its expression in varying levels and spheres of affirmative action. To understand this logic, a closer look at the concept of justice and at the nature of the commitment to it may well be in order.

The centrality of Justice to the Muslim historical consciousness flows from its place in the Muslim historical community. Both in its constitutive principle and in its goal-orientation or purposiveness, the *umma* of *tawḥīd* contains the core value of Justice as a constituent in the one case and as a component in the other. Emanating from *Tawḥīd,* Justice *(al-'Adl)* as Truth *(al-Ḥaqq)* are themselves Divine Attributes, expressions of the *asmā' al-ḥusnā* that ought to be reflected in the Righteous Order.[7] Bridging the gap between the Is and the Ought in a given historical situation falls upon the Community which, by virtue of its constitution and its direction, is given to these principles. The nature of the relationship between the personal and the collective in Islam underlies the dynamics of this task. While the burden of the historical responsibility falls on the Community as a whole, the Muslim is not released of his share of it. His accountability remains a personal one however and unlike the collectivity, its verdict transcends history. The failure of the Community is paid for in history, while the struggle of the individual Muslim is not contingent on its historical outcome and its recompense is meted out in handsome measure on the Day of Judgement.

Conversely put, the pursuit of Justice is a duty incumbent on the collectivity and as such it ought to be discharged by its entrusted agents, or by the organs of the Community. Failing that the resistance of oppression and the checking of injustice becomes a personal responsibility incumbent on every able Muslim, man or woman. This position has been formalized in Muslim Jurisprudence where the scope and limits of the Muslim's obligations are meticulously defined and elaborated. It distinguishes two sets of categories, the collective and the personal duties, respectively the *farḍ kifāya* and the *farḍ 'ain.* The distinction is not solely based on the nature of the duty in question but it also takes into account the extent to which it is observed in society at a given moment. If a collective obligation dischargeable on behalf of the majority by an entrusted minority is abused or neglected then this obligation reverts to the majority. As such it becomes a *farḍ 'ain,* a personal responsibility. Consistent with the Muslim's social conscience, the commitment to justice cannot be abandoned on the pretext of a slack, degenerate or powerless Organization. Wherever *tawḥīd* inspires the heart, its ideals continue to motivate a pattern of devotion that includes a commitment to Justice for the love of God and Good.

In a conscience saturated with *taqwā,* it is the devotion itself that counts, i.e. the endeavour to bring about justice and not its immediate results. Ultimately, the Muslim *knows* that the yields will not be lost and that the reward for his endeavours are assured. To him, it is the Ultimate Court of Appeal that counts and in its judgement lies a justice that can be matched by no other. With this conviction and assurance, there are always Muslims, acting as individuals and groups, who are prepared to defy countless odds and take it upon themselves to right a wrong or to take a stand against a rampant form of oppression. Perhaps the most single outstanding example of this stance in contemporary times is embodied in the heroic stance of the Afghan *mujāhidīn* whose resistance to the formidable power of the Soviets and their puppets over the past several years has assumed legendary proportions. The turn of the Muslim Resistance in South Lebanon and the *intifada* in occupied Palestine against the Israeli occupation and in the face of the threat of yet another annexation is another case in point. Brutalities are not the preserve of foreign troops or of invading forces alone, an oppression can be practised by one's own people as in the case of 'Alawite Syria where the ruling oligarchy nearly wiped a historical city out of existence in 1981 in an attempt to eradicate its opponents. In these examples and many others one recurrently encounters the spectacle of strongly motivated individuals and groups set on a course that is doomed by all worldly standards. In every case, they are prompted by an unfailing faith in the justice of their Cause *and in the justice of their Lord.*

Such events can only be understood in the context of the nature of the commitment to Justice and in its connection with *tawḥīd.* What distinguishes this commitment among Muslims – for after all it is a universal commitment ingrained in the nature of human creation, or in the human *fiṭra* – is the fact and belief that worldly justice is rooted in a transcendental Justice and that the commitment to its pursuit in the Here-and-Now is the corollary to a conviction in its redemption in the Hereafter. Throughout Muslim history this conviction has had its practical social implications for the conduct of individuals and groups. In every case however, the scope and limitations of this commitment is a function of the given situation. It is only in extreme situations, where the alternatives to righting a wrong *(ẓulm)* and checking an Injustice are totally denied, that the pursuit of Justice comes to be equated with sacrifice of one's earthly life. Only then is the ethos of *infāq* which is the warp and weft of the cohesive Community at every level of its social organization, transformed into an embattled *jihād* and climax into its ultimate expression.

If the baffled observer fails to grasp the integrality of justice to the Muslim sensibility and is unable to appreciate the cluster of attitudes in which it is embedded, an entire dimension of contemporary political reality in Muslim societies will continue to elude understanding. He will throw up his hands in despair and, more ominously, react in consternation, not necessarily because of an inherent 'senselessness' in a given situation, but as an expression of his own frustration in failing to see the meaning of it all. The ambiguity and the absence of meaning are to be found in the reader, not in the text and no amount of detail and information can help to induce comprehension if the constraint lies in a mental/psychological blockage. This is a comment on the banalities and dangers attendant on a prevailing tradition of political analysis that focuses on considerations of power and stability while ignoring the substantive dimensions of both. Such analysis moreover computes the detail and the dents but stops short of ascertaining the causes and the results. It is ultimately hampered in its understanding because it fails to relate the parts to the whole. This understanding calls for an appreciation of the substance of Islamic Justice.

Contrary to revolutionary ideals that are often sought but rarely defined, Islamic Justice is no vague, diffuse or elusive ideal. Any illusion about the arbitrariness of its pursuit should be dispelled. The Just Order is pursued as a definable quest. Its details and workings may well vary from one historical setting to another and from generation to generation so as to accommodate the variables inherent in the changing human condition. The fundamentals and contours of this Order however, remain essentially constant and serve as milestones and guides in the perpetual challenge of organizing human societies. That modicum of permanence and stability is plausible in view of the fact that worldly Justice is derived from Divine Justice and the fact that the Just Social Order is anchored in the matrix of *tawḥīd*. Indeed, the relative only assumes its meaning and direction when it is related to a standing order of Right and Truth where the Source may be transcendental, but the scope and reach are imminent in Creation. This is of the essence of Justice and the Just Order. In the perspective of *tawḥīd* moreover, the latter is more than plausible; it is fully capable of substantiation in the light of the Divinely prescribed ethical-legal Code known as the *sharī'a*. Its realizability is in fact assured in view of historical precedent.

Simply stated, Islamic Justice is not Utopia. Nor are the tracts of jurists abstract gropings to regulate society in a world of formalities. Islamic Jurisprudence is embedded in that transcendental value-system which enables it to meet the needs of change in society from a position of strength; ideally, it is in a position to lead and instruct such change, not simply to react and keep up with it. Furthermore, the standards that inform the legal code are the same as those which give rise to the great social movements that mobilize the potentials for change and reform in society. In the *sharī'a* the tensions between the legal and the moral are resolved because both are derived from an epistemological and morphological order that integrates the inner and the outer life. Consequently, the legal draws its binding force from its appeal and its relevance to the inner order while the moral has its concrete consequences for social conduct. Both are integral to the Just Order *(al-'Adl)*. The external parameters of this Society are set by the *sharī'a,* or the Law, and they constitute the *ḥudūd,* literally the bounds of socio-legality which must not be transgressed. Beyond that, and within such bounds, the substance and the fibre of social morality is drawn from a pervasive ethos rooted in *tawḥīd* and cultivating the pursuit of righteousness. Accordingly, Muslims are urged to join together in protesting all forms of tyranny *(ẓulm)* and oppression (*baghī* or *ṭughyān*) in the name of a Just Order. The principles of the latter have been systematically elaborated in the great works of Islamic Jurisprudence. The basis for this elaboration is found in the Recorded Guidance of the Qur'ān and in the example of the *sunna* of the Prophet (peace be upon him). As the first Islamic Society in Madina was modelled on these sources, it has continued to this day to inspire movements and individuals in their search for a Just and Righteous Order.

To many Muslims today it would seem that an effective check against the humiliation, corruption and oppression in their respective societies can only be found in a comprehensive code that is at once legal and moral. The *sharī'a* alone seems to qualify for these needs. Objectively, only a system stemming from the metaphysics of *tawḥīd* can be immune to the bias which inheres in the human/social condition. While the pursuit of Justice will generally tend to fall short of the ideal, the system which incorporates its principles and sets the premises for the practice should not. In the *sharī'a,* Justice meets its absolute standards because it is derived from *tawḥīd,* i.e. from the Absolute. The relative aspect is left to its pursuit. Conversely, where Muslims are in a majority, it is only natural to expect the *sharī'a* to be the only effective social code for that society for it is the only code persons subscribing to *tawḥīd* can relate to and accept.

To further elucidate the place of the *sharī'a* for the Just Society in Muslim perceptions, an analogy may be drawn from another area of the historical experience of the *umma.* In the arts of Islam, in the geometric and the floral patterns of its arabesques, there is that pervasive motif that relates form to content in such a way as to achieve the ideal Concordance. Islamic architecture too, is concerned with conceiving a functional structure which at the same time authentically reflects the spirit of the Community in the principles and ideals of its Faith. So it is with society at large. In the architectonics of the Just Order the same concern with consistency and coherence prevails. It becomes urgent to reconcile the outer forms of the Community manifest in its legal order with the inner dimension of a public ethos modelled in its own spirituality and identity. Any attempt to impose an order not sustained by its moral underpinnings constitutes an incongruity, or a deviation that is justly deemed by its victims to be a transgression against the Just Order. Likewise, to ignore or neglect the need for developing the institutions in society in accordance with its prevailing innate beliefs and ethical premises is ultimately damaging both to morale and to social organization alike. It perpetuates an unwarranted dualism or split in society which stunts the Community and offends its sense of identity.

Throughout much of the Muslim world today there prevails a sense of Wrong induced by what is seen as a flagrant violation of

Justice. What in the realm of art may be judged as 'ugly' for violating standards of beauty, becomes outrageous in society for transgressing the bounds of righteousness. In view of its comprehensive nature moreover, *tawḥīd*-sprung morality renders that which impinges on the sense of right and wrong in society ultimately an impingement on its system of Justice too. Questions of legitimacy and legality are inseparable. Here too the analogy between art and society comes to an end.

A Justice that cannot be brought about in the face of persistent recalcitrance and abuse would indeed be a lame Justice. It is then reduced to a vain refuge for the helpless and a banner for hypocrisy. In the context of a Muslim world-view it has no place. The hallmark of the Muslim is a sincerity *(ikhlāṣ)* born of the pure devotion to God in *taqwā*. The meaning of life is sought in this devotion and service and the trials and tribulations in the process are a test of his *ikhlāṣ*. The dedication to procuring the means of assuring the Just Order is itself a measure of the dedication to this Order. It is doubly enjoined: first, upon the Community as a measure of self-defence and of upholding the ideals for which it stands and, second, upon Muslims acting individually or as groups in the same dual capacity. In the world-view of Islam, the means are sanctified for they partake of the same Just Order to which they contribute and of which they are a part. Here there is no room for a dispensation where the ends justify the means. In view of their Source, the standards of Good and Right are universal and immutable, and they apply as such to both means and ends. There is nothing innately evil – or good – about 'power' *(al-sulṭān)* for example; to the extent that power is indispensable for bringing about Justice it is 'good' and 'right' and in its exercise it must accordingly subscribe to a hierarchy of values. Throughout their history, Muslims could not afford to be indifferent to power without imperilling the balance of their fate and forfeiting their prescribed responsibility as a '*khair umma*' (the best of nations).

It is in this perspective that *jihād* has been ingrained in the historical consciousness of Muslims. To the extent that it provides the means for the Community to fulfil its purpose and realize Justice, its underlying logic and thrust enshrine the same principles which permeate this consciousness. The following summary of ideas should therefore serve as a convenient point of recapitulation. At the same time they highlight the premises for *jihād* as the third basic concept of Islamic socio-political thought and action.

- An affirmative, action-oriented attitude to life is the norm.
- In this orientation, values and sanctions are as a rule absolute. Commitment is beyond compromise because it is drawn from the initial pledge of devotion in the *shahāda*.
- The nature of accountability is ultimately individual and personal. Temporally however, it has its historical consequences for the Community.
- In view of his *khilāfa,* or vicegerency, man is charged with enjoining what is right and rectifying the wrong. Setting up the Just Order in this world is not only possible and desirable, but it is positively a duty and a responsibility which exacts accountability.
- Change is a function of a person's will and resolution. Change in society is basically a function of a change in morality. Hence, social regeneration, i.e. external or outer reform is rooted in the renewal of Faith. The latter spells an inner regeneration which affects the heart *(al-nafs)* and the mind *(al-'aql)* in its perceptions and ways of thought.
- The righteous life is contingent on the righteous society. All moral strivings in Muslim Society are bound to have their social consequences. A good Muslim does not realize himself in the hermitage but in society. The good society is not born out of a state of mystical elation, but in the process of historical realization.
- Throughout, life is perceived as a continuum with reward and retribution distributed along the line. Divine or Absolute Justice is meted out in recompense only in the Hereafter. So the Muslim strives in this world with his eyes set on the Hereafter. He is sustained through all his ordeals and in the face of the setbacks he encounters by his unshakeable trust in the Justice of the Almighty and in the Truth of His Promise.

In the above context it is easy to understand how *jihād,* for a devout Muslim, can become a code of life. Its corollary, as mentioned earlier, is *infāq* and its ultimate expression is in *istishhād.* With this in mind, let us briefly probe into the assumptions of *jihād.* As a compound concept, *jihād* denotes the striving in the Way of God. It entails bearing hardship with patience and fortitude on the one hand and persevering in the Cause of Justice and Truth on the other. In this sense, *jihād* is contingent on a set of attitudes and orientations subsumed under a willingness to give of all that one values starting with one's wealth and ending with oneself. That willingness to expend is the other side of the coin for a readiness to part with all that is near and dear in this world for the love of God. In the *ḥadīth* it is said that the believer is not truly a believer unless and until his love for Allah (SWT) and His Prophet (peace be upon him) is greater than his love for himself. The corollary to this attitude is a deliberate and conscious orientation to the Hereafter in all one's actions. This orientation transcends but does not neglect the Here-and-Now where the norm of communal solidarity further tests the believer's resolve to measure up to the injunction to 'love for his brother what he loves for himself'. This capacity to live up to the standards of selfless *infāq* calls for a scale of values and priorities which clearly gives precedence to the Unseen and enduring over the tangible and ephemeral. Nothing short of an unwavering faith in God and an unremitting trust in His Promise, in Truth, could inculcate such a scale. Not surprisingly, the belief in *al-ghaib* is the Crown and Pillar of *īmān.* Seen in this light, the Pillars of the Faith are all means to an end (as well as devotions in their own right): they all prepare the Muslim for this role of *jihād* and they nurture the Community that can provide the human context and support for this purpose of the Just Striving.

Furthermore, in postulating the willingness to give without flinching, *jihād* sets the tone for the individual and the Community. If sincerity or *ikhlāṣ* is the hallmark for the one, righteousness is the brand for the other. The manifest destination of the human vicegerency on Earth is to expend of one's energies, faculties and the resources placed at one's command by God in *taskhīr* so as to establish the course of a Civilization in this world which incorporates the elements of Right: Truth and Justice. This constitutes the legitimate objective of the Just Striving. Even where *jihād* may appear to come to no immediate fruition, Muslims are still pledged to the effort which is seen as a winning investment all the same. As was the case with the commitment to Justice, their commitment here to an ideal of sacrifice remains unabated. Here too, their logic is inscrutable for it is rooted in an implacable faith nurtured in the metaphysics of *tawḥīd.* The fruits they miss in this world they *know* they will reap all the more in the Next World *(al-ākhira).* And here comparisons crumble to the advantage of the latter: however rich the harvest of this world, be it in the success of Civilizations and Empires, it is a harvest that is inevitably subject to shrivelling, rot and decomposition; not so the enduring harvest of the Hereafter. What the brilliant and perpicacious historian of our times, Arnold Toynbee, missed when he wrote about the phenomenal expansion of Islam at its inception, was the ethos of dedication that inspired and accompanied the rise of the Community and the Faith. Worldly glory was not the end of the 'Warriors of Allah' when they set out on their conquests bent on achieving one of the two 'glorious ends', victory or *shahāda* (being slain in the Way of God). It was the Pleasure and the Favour of God which they sought. It was in striving for this intangible end that they came by worldly success – which was in turn seen as a manifest sign, a 'downpayment' on the promise of God to those who submit their will to His Will and commit all they value in His Way.

The frame of mind of the devoted Muslim bred and fed on the ethics of *tawḥīd* is to cherish that which is beyond material measure. In undertaking *jihād,* it is *wajhullāh,* the Countenance of God, which he seeks, and in earning the Pleasure and Favour of His Master and Cherisher of the Worlds, his self-satisfaction and inner contentment are assured. The serene and contented self, *al-nafs al-rāḍiya al-marḍīya,* and the self which has found its innermost sense of peace, *al-nafs al-muṭma'inna* are anchored in that infinite and unassailable source from which they draw. It is *riḍā' Allāh* the pleasure of Allah, which constitutes the ultimate goal and prize in the devotee's arduous pursuits. This theme aptly invites a few closing remarks on the subject of *istishhād.*

If *jihād* is a prescription for the Muslim's worldly life, then *istishhād,* which is the reflexive form of *'shahāda',* is best described as the Code for defeating or circumventing death. *Istishhād* is the voluntary act of submitting one's life unto its very end in pursuit of the pleasure of God. Simply, it is dying, or being slain in the active pursuit of fulfilling God's Will on Earth. It is the ultimate attestation of one's commitment to an unswerving devotion in His Service. While normally the run of a Muslim's life is full of opportunities for devoted self-exertion in the ways of righteousness by giving of his time, wealth and effort, it is only rarely that he will be called upon to attest to his devotion by giving up life itself. There will however always be those situations where the only scope for self-exertion in the Cause of Righteousness and God is in staking one's life. Sometimes, merely upholding a Word of Truth in the face of a tyrant will be an invitation to persecution and prosecution. At other times, the only recourse to checking repression and defending Justice and Right is to rally to the battlefield and prepare for martyrdom. 'Permission (to fight) is given to those against whom war is wrongfully waged – and verily God has indeed the power to succour them – those who have been driven from their homes against all right for no other reason than their saying "Our Sustainer is God". . . ' (22: 39, 40). Such is an injunction that compellingly resounds in the heart and soul of every Muslim who has taken to heart the lessons of the Qur'ān and the *sunna*. 'And how could you refuse to fight in the cause of God and of the utterly helpless men and women and children who are crying "O, our Sustainer, lead us forth to freedom out of this land whose people are oppressors, and raise for us out of Thy grace, a protector, and raise for us out of Thy grace, one who will bring us succour"' (4: 74). To those who have been initiated in the Qur'ānic code of Honour and Dignity, affirming and reinforcing an innate code inherent in human creation by virtue of *fiṭra,* such appeals goad the Muslim social conscience whenever and wherever it is confronted with the spectre of destitution. Where there is no established Authority to speak up for this conscience and to effectively organize for enacting its Will, individuals and groups will not fail to fall back on their own resources however limited or even pathetic they might be.

In the Muslim ethos martyrdom is a dynamic and active ideal. The renunciation of the joys and pleasures of this life in favour of the Promise to come is not an act of self-denial, nor is it a deliberate self-infliction of hardship and suffering for itself. There is nothing to suggest a Hellenistic asceticism, or a Christian or Hindu mysticism in the choice of the Muslim *mujāhid*. His renunciation of this world is not in negation of this world. Rather, this renunciation is simultaneously an act of denunciation and an act of affirmation: a denunciation of immorality and injustice and an affirmation of the necessity and the possibility of setting things in the way of Justice and Right. Here again, it is action and not meditation that is emphasized. The virtuous life is the righteous life and righteousness is not a given state of grace, but it is a way of life that calls for striving and pursuit. A human being is born into an active role from the very start. He is a born 'doer'. But the *homo faber* in Islam has his roots in the *homo sapiens,* whereby knowledge is taken to incorporate faith; and indeed, the link is integral, not assumed (30: 56). However, both the *homo faber* and the *homo sapiens* are rooted in the ideal of the integrated and the whole human being who constitute an integral whole, the *homo concord*.

It follows that Islamically, the most congenial system or order of governance, is that which assures the basic freedoms of expression and life. It affords the Muslim the maximum opportunity for self-fulfilment through devoting his God-given life, talents and resources to the benefit of a humane and flourishing Civilization. In such a society, the Muslim's *jihād* is an indisputable source of strength for it will make of him a member more willing to put into society than to take out of it. It will also make of him a reliable support and an advocate to be reckoned with on the side of the Good and the Right and the Just against the inevitable undermining forces that are at work in all societies. Conversely, the least congenial social system or government from the Muslim point of view is that which flouts human values and denies the basic freedoms of expression and action. In this setting the opportunities for self-affirmation in the cause of Right and Goodness are reduced to the marginal. Instead of self-exertion in the task of constructive edification in a just civic order, the Muslim will be engaged in the strife to attain and defend these basic rights. His energies and resources will be spent in resisting and combating the forces of evil and oppression. His *jihād* life-span is more likely to be brutishly short and exact its price in terms of human affliction, suffering and deprivation. Nonetheless, the devoted Muslim will gladly pay the toll of self-exertion in the circumstances and, in the process, he will draw on an incorruptible and inexhaustible fund for his moral fortitude and endurance. In the circumstances too, it will make him anticipate the *shahāda* of *istishhād* as an honour to be coveted and an aspiration to be fulfilled.

On this note we may conclude with two observations on the *shahāda* as the beginning and the end of the Muslim historical consciousness. First, as shown above, *istishhād* is the natural sequel to the ethics of the Just Striving, and in this sense, it constitutes the crowning and consummation of the ideal of *jihād*. The Qur'ān teaches that this ultimate act of renouncing life is nothing short of an assurance of its conservation, a definite confirmation of its blissful immortality.[8] The second point calls for a reflection on the affinity between the original act of faith subsumed under the *shahāda* and *istishhād,* which is also referred to as *shahāda*. The *shahīd* is one who lays down his life in this latter act of *shahāda.* In fact, all these terms relate to an act of bearing witness. The relationship is not accidental. In the first *shahāda,* the believer is self-pledged by way of an uttered profession to the total surrender in devotion to the Will of God. It is his testimony of recognition and acknowledgement of his Creator and Sustainer. In the ultimate *shahāda,* the Muslim comes to confirm his original pledge by way of an irrevocable act/deed of faith and will. In the first *shahāda,* the pledge was to live up to a commitment, in the ultimate *shahāda* the Muslim has proved truthful to his pledge. As the *shāhid,* the one who bears witness, becomes a *shahīd,* a martyr in the Way of God, there is literally an inflexion of the verb whereby the original witness and testimony is intensified. The *shahīd* has literally borne witness upon himself of the truthfulness of his original intent, or *niyya,* unto the very end. This glorious affinity is made explicit in the Qur'ān. In the faith of the Muslim and in his way of life, the primal act of piety converges with the ultimate act of piety. A *shahāda* borne and fulfilled is the climax of *tawḥīd.*

> **Among the believers are men who have been true to their Covenant with God: and among them are such that have already redeemed their pledge by death, and such as yet await its fulfilment without having changed (their resolve) in the least. (33: 23)**

. . . and (this) to the end that God might mark out those who have attained to faith, and choose from among you such as (with their lives) bear witness to the truth . . . (3: 140)

Truthful is God Almighty: *ṣadaqa Allāh al-'aẓīm.*

Notes and References

1. See Chapter 3.

2. *Qibla* is the direction which Muslims face in *ṣalāt,* i.e. the Ka'ba. *'Wajh'* literally means face and *'ittijāh'*, direction; together they denote orientation. All are mentioned in the Qur'ān in the context of the *Umma* (2: 143–9). Also cf. Chapter 3.

3. The *sharī'a* is an ethical-legal Code based in *tawḥīd* and derived from the Qur'ān and *sunna* and underlies the corpus of Islamic Jurisprudence *(fiqh)*. See below.

4. Literally deliberation or consultation and taking counsel for *shūrā*, and studious self-application or methodological intellectual exertion to devise alternatives and new solutions from given principles.

5. Most notable in this respect perhaps is the work of 14th century historian and sociologist Ibn Khaldūn in his *Prolegomena.*

6. See Chapter 2 on *Zakāt.*

7. See Chapter 1.

8. E.g. *sūras* 2: 154; 3: 169–71 and 157; 22: 58, 59.

Appendix 1

Bismillah ar-Rahman ar-Rahim

'In the Name of God, Most Gracious, Most Merciful'

Islam from its Sources: Themes from the Qur'ān

Conception of God:

Say Allah is One, Allah is the eternally besought
He Begetteth not nor has He begotten
Nor is there anything the like unto Him. (112: 1–4)

And your God is one God
There is no God but He
The most Gracious, the most Merciful. (2: 163)

Allah – There is no God but He –
the Living, the Self-subsisting, Eternal:
no slumber can seize Him nor sleep
His are all things in the heavens and on earth.
Who is it that can intercede in His presence
except as He permits?
He knows what (appears to his creatures as)
before or after or behind them;
nor shall they compass aught of His knowledge
except as He wills
His throne extends over the Heavens and the Earth
and He feels no fatigue in guarding and preserving them
for He is the Most High, the Supreme (in glory). (2: 255)

Say: To whom belongs all that is in the Heavens
and on the Earth? Say: To Allah;
He has inscribed upon Himself (the rule of) Mercy . . . (6: 12)

No vision can grasp Him, but His vision is over all vision
(He is above all comprehension) but is acquainted
with all things. (6: 103)

When My servants ask you concerning Me: (instruct them that)
I am indeed close (to them):
I listen to the prayer of every suppliant
when he calls upon Me:
Let them also with a will respond to My call
and believe in Me –
That they may walk in the Right Way. (2: 186)

Call on Him with fear and longing (anticipation):
for the Mercy of Allah is always near
to those who do good. (7: 56)

If God touches you with affliction
none can remove it but He;
if He touches you with happiness
it is He (alone) who has power over all things. (6: 17)

Now has come unto you a Messenger from amidst yourselves
solicitous of your burdens, caring for you,
to believers most compassionate and merciful;
but if they turn away say: God sufficeth me
there is no God save He, in Him alone do I trust . . . (9: 128–9)

O Humankind, heed your Lord
who has created you from a single self
and of it created its mate,
and of them twain
has spread forth countless men and women. (4: 1)

O Humankind, the Messenger has come to you
with the Truth from your Lord: so believe in Him
It is best for you;
But if you reject faith, (then know that)
To God belong all things
in the heavens and on earth:
(Your ingratitude will not detract an iota
from His dominion) –
God is All-Knowing, All-Wise. (4: 170)

The Mission of the Prophet

Verily We have sent you in Truth:
as bearer of glad tidings and a warner;
(But you are not accountable for those
who reject your mission). (2: 119)

And We have sent you as a Messenger
to (instruct) mankind;
and suffice God for a witness. (4: 79)

Say: O humankind, I am sent unto you,
all of you, as the Messenger of Allah,
to Whom belongs the Dominion of the Heavens
and of Earth; There is no god save He,
it is He who gives both life and death. (7: 158)

Say: O humankind, Truth has come unto you
from your Lord; so whosoever is guided
his guidance is (a light) unto himself
and whosoever strays does so to his own detriment;
surely I am not your keeper. (10: 108)

Now has come unto you a messenger from amidst yourselves
solicitous of your burdens, caring for you,
to believers most compassionate and merciful;
but if they turn away say: God sufficeth me
there is no God save He, in Him alone do I trust . . . (9: 128-9)

O Humankind, the Messenger has come to you
with the Truth from your Lord: so believe in Him
It is best for you;
But if you reject faith, (then know that)
To God belong all things
in the heavens and on earth:
(Your ingratitude will not detract an iota
from His dominion) –
God is All-Knowing, All-Wise (4: 170)

Concept of 'The Book': 'The True Religion'

And this is a Book which We have sent down
as a Blessing;
So follow it in righteousness and take heed:
That you may receive Mercy. (6: 155)

The word of thy Lord hath been completed
in Truth and in Justice;
none can change His words:
Verily He is the all-Hearing the all-Knowing. (6: 115)

If you were to follow the common run of those on earth
they will surely lead you away from the way of God:
They follow naught but conjecture
(and conjecture is no substitute for Truth)
Your Lord knows best who strays from His way
and He knows best who they are
that bide His Guidance. (6: 116, 117)

This Day have I Perfected your religion for you
Completed My Favour upon you
and have sanctioned (chosen, approved and confirmed)
for you
Islam as The Religion. (5: 3)

There has come to you from Allah a Light
and a perspicuous Book
wherewith Allah guides all who seek His
good pleasure to ways of Peace and Safety;
and leads them out of darkness, with His will,
unto the Light –
and guides them to a Path that is Straight. (5: 15, 16)

We send down in the Qur'ān that which is
a Healing and a Mercy to those who believe;
To those who wrong themselves,
it causes nothing but loss upon loss. (17: 82)

This – without doubt – is the Book!
Wherein – without doubt – is Guidance:
To those who fear God. (2: 2)

Concept of the Resurrection: Al-Ba'th (Restoration to Life After Death)

It is Allah who begins the process of creation
Then restores it;
Then shall ye be brought back unto Him. (30: 11)

O Mankind! If ye have a doubt about the
resurrection (then consider this)
that We created you out of dust, then out of sperm,
then out of a leech-like clot, then out of a morsel of flesh,
partly formed and partly unformed –
that We may make manifest unto you (Our Power)
and clarify to you (The signs of your own Creation) –
and We cause whom We will to rest in the wombs for
an appointed term, then do We bring you
out as babes, then (foster you) that ye may
reach your age of full strength; and some of
you are called to die, and some are sent back
to the feeblest old age, so that they know naught
after having known (much).
And further you see the earth barren
and lifeless.
But when We pour down rain upon it,

it is stirred (to life), it swells
and puts forth every kind of splendid growth
in pairs.

This is so because it is Allah who is the Truth, the Reality:
it is He who gives life to the dead
and it is He who has power over all things. (22: 5–6)

It is He who brings out the living from the dead
and brings out the dead from the living
. . . who gives life to the earth
after its death.
And thus shall you be brought out from the dead. (30: 19)

Is not He who created the heavens and earth
able to create the like thereof?!
Yes, indeed! For He is the Creator supreme
of skill and knowledge infinite. (36: 81)

See they not how Allah originates creation
then restores it: Truly that is easy for Allah.
Say: Travel through the earth and see
how Allah did originate the creation –
so too will Allah produce the later creation. (29: 18–19)

Blessed is He who sent down the Criterion
to His servant
That it may be an Admonition
to all creatures. (25: 1)

O Mankind! Heed your Lord
for the coming of the Hour shall be of an awesome magnitude.

That Day, you shall see it,
when every mother giving suck – dazed-stricken
shall abandon her suckling babe
and every pregnant female shall drop her load
unformed
You shall see mankind as in a drunken riot
yet not drunk –
dreadful then will be the wrath of God. (22: 1–2)

That Day the heaven shall be rent asunder
beclouded; and angels shall be sent forth
descending in ranks. (25: 25)

It will be no more than a single blast
when lo! They will all be brought up before Us. (36: 53)

That Day the dominion of Right and Truth
shall be wholly for Allah, Most Merciful;
It will be a day of dire difficulty
for the misbelievers. (25: 26)

Then on that Day – not a soul will be wronged
in the least: and ye shall but be repaid
the meeds of your past deeds. (36: 54; cf. 21: 47)

The Balance that Day will be true
to a nicety . . . (7: 8–9; cf. 99: 7–8)

And verily the Hour will come
of this there is no doubt;
nor is there any doubt
that Allah will raise up all who are in the graves. (22: 7)

Concept of the Noble Sanctuary Baitullāh al-Ḥarām, the Qibla

Remember We made the House
a place of Assembly for humankind
And a Refuge of safety;
(So) Take the station of Abraham
as a place of prayer:
We covenanted with Abraham and Ismail
that they should sanctify My House
for those who compass it round
or use it as a retreat, or
bow in prostration therein. (2: 125)

And remember Abraham and Ismail
raised the foundations of the House
(with this prayer): Our Lord
accept from us this service
for You are the All-Hearing, the All-Knowing:
Our Lord, make of us Muslims (as of this day and always)
bowing to Your will
and of our progeny a people who are Muslim,
bowing to Your will. (2: 128)

From whencesoever you start forth
Turn your face in the direction
of the Sacred Mosque:
'tis indeed the Truth from Thy Lord –
God is not unmindful
of what you do. (2: 149)

. . . and wheresoever you are
Set your face There (in that direction). (2: 150)

Concept of the Umma (Community) in Islam

You are the best of peoples
evolved for humankind: (for)
Enjoining what is right
Forbidding what is wrong
and Believing in God. (3: 110)

Let there arise out of you
an *Umma*
inviting to all that is good
enjoining what is right
forbidding what is wrong:
such are they who truly prosper. (3: 104)

Thus have We made of you
an *Umma* justly balanced
that you might be Witnesses
over the nations
and that the Messenger

might be a Witness
over you yourselves. (2: 143)

Attitude to Guidance

O Humankind, there has indeed come to you
evident proof from your Lord;
Verily we have revealed to you
a light that is manifest:
As for those who believe in Allah
and hold fast unto Him
them will He admit to his Mercy and Grace
and them will He guide to Himself
by a Straight Path. (4: 174)

This is a Clarification to humankind
a Guidance and an Instruction
to those who take heed. (3: 138)

Say: O People of the Book,
Why reject ye the signs of God:
God is Himself witness to all ye do. (3: 98)

That is Allah your Lord
there is no god save He
the Creator of all things:
then worship Him alone
for verily He alone hath power
to dispose of all things. (6: 102)

Now have come to you from your Lord
eye-opening proofs:
If any will see it is to his own good
if any will be blind it will be to his own (harm);
I am not here to watch over your doings
It is not for you (O Muḥammad)
to set them on the right path; but
Allah sets on the right path whom He pleases. (2: 272)

O you who do believe, believe in God and His Messenger
and the Scripture which He has sent down to His Messenger,
and the Scripture which He has sent down to those before
(him).
(4: 136)

Attitude to Guidance/Response to Guidance

There is no compulsion in religion:
Truth stands out clear from error,
whosoever renounces evil and believes in Allah
has grasped the most trustworthy clasp
that is indissoluble;
Verily Allah hears and knows all things,

Allah is the protector of those who believe,
From the depths of darkness
He will lead them forth into the Light. (2: 256, 257)

Say (O you who believe): Verily my Lord
has guided me onto a way that is straight –
A Religion Upright;
The cult of Abraham, the true and pure,
for (certainly) he was not of those who
joined others to God.

Say (O you who believe);
My prayer and my rites,
My life and my death
All (in their entirety)
are for Allah Alone

Lord of the Worlds
No partner has He,
This am I commanded –
and I am the first of those who bow in submission. (6: 161–3)

Say: Shall I take my protector any other than Allah:
the Maker of Heavens and Earth?

. . . Say Nay – But I am commanded to be
the first of those who bow to Allah (in Islam)
And do not yourself be of those who join others to God
(*Mushrikīn*).
(6: 14)

Appendix 2

Authenticity of the Qur'an: How it Came to be Written*

Thanks to its undisputed authenticity, the text of the Qur'an holds a unique place among the books of Revelation, shared neither by the Old nor the New Testament. In the first two sections of this work, a review was made of the alterations undergone by the Old Testament and the Gospels before they were handed down to us in the form we know today. The same is not true for the Qur'an for the simple reason that it was written down at the time of the Prophet; we shall see how it came to be written, i.e. the process involved.

In this context, the differences separating the Qur'an from the Bible are in no way due to questions essentially concerned with date. Such questions are constantly put forward by certain people without regard to the circumstances prevailing at the time when the Judeo-Christian and the Qur'anic Revelations were written; they have an equal disregard for the circumstances surrounding the transmission of the Qur'an to the Prophet. It is suggested that a Seventh century text had more likelihood of coming down to us unaltered than other texts that are as many as fifteen centuries older. This comment, although correct, does not constitute a sufficient reason; it is made more to excuse the alterations made in the Judeo-Christian texts in the course of centuries than to underline the notion that the text of the Qur'an, which was more recent, had less to fear from being modified by man.

---

*Dr. Maurice Bucaille, *The Bible, The Qur'an and Science – The Holy Scriptures Examined in the Light of Modern Knowledge*, Translated from the French by Alastair Pannell and the Author. Third Edition, Revised and Expanded (Seghers, Paris – 1982). Excerpt cited here is taken, with kind permission, from edition published by the North American Trust Publications.

In the case of the Old Testament, the sheer number of authors who tell the same story, plus all the revisions carried out on the text of certain books from the pre-Christian era, constitute as many reasons for inaccuracy and contradiction. As for the Gospels, nobody can claim that they invariably contain faithful accounts of Jesus's words or a description of his actions strictly in keeping with reality. We have seen how successive versions of the texts showed a lack of definite authenticity and moreover that their authors were not eyewitnesses.

Also to be underlined is the distinction to be made between the Qur'an, a book of written Revelation, and the hadiths, collections of statements concerning the actions and sayings of Muhammad. Some of the Prophet's companions started to write them down from the moment of his death. As an element of human error could have slipped in, the collection had to be resumed later and subjected to rigorous criticism so that the greatest credit is in practise given to documents that came along after Muhammad. Their authenticity varies, like that of the Gospels. Not a single Gospel was written down at the time of Jesus (they were all written long after his earthly mission had come to an end), and not a single collection of hadiths was compiled during the time of the Prophet.

The situation is very different for the Qur'an. As the Revelation progressed, the Prophet and the believers following him recited the text by heart and it was also written down by the scribes in his following. It therefore starts off with two elements of authenticity that the Gospels do not possess. This continued up to the Prophet's death. At a time when not everybody could write, but everyone was able to recite, recitation afforded a considerable advantage because of the double-checking possible when the definitive text was compiled.

The Qur'anic Revelation was made by Archangel Gabriel to Muhammad. It took place over a period of more than twenty years of the Prophet's life, beginning with the first verses of Sura 96, then resuming after a three-year break for a long period of twenty years up to the death of the Prophet in 632 A.D., i.e. ten years before Hegira and ten years after Hegira.[1]

The following was the first Revelation (sura 96, verses 1 to 5)[2] :

"Read: In the name of thy Lord who created,
Who created man from something which clings
Read! Thy Lord is the most Noble
Who taught by the pen
Who taught man what he did not know."

Professor Hamidullah notes in the Introduction to his French translation of the Qur'an that one of the themes of this first Revelation was the 'praise of the pen as a means of human knowledge' which would 'explain the Prophet's concern for the preservation of the Qur'an in writing.'

Texts formally prove that long before the Prophet left Makka for Madina (i.e. long before Hegira), the Qur'anic text so far revealed had been written down. We shall see how the Qur'an is authentic in this. We know that Muhammad and the Believers who surrounded him were accustomed to reciting the revealed text from memory. It is therefore inconceivable for the Qur'an to refer to facts that did not square with reality because the latter could so easily be checked with people in the Prophet's following, by asking the authors of the transcription.

Four suras dating from a period prior to Hegira refer to the writing down of the Qur'an before the Prophet left Makka in 622 (sura 80, verses 11 to 16):

"By no means! Indeed it is a message of instruction
Therefore whoever wills, should remember
On leaves held in honor
Exalted, purified
In the hands of scribes
Noble and pious."

Yusuf Ali, in the commentary to his translation, 1934, wrote that when the Revelation of this sura was made, forty-two or forty-five others had been written and were kept by Muslims in Makka (out of a total of 114).

– Sura 85, verses 21 and 22:
"Nay, this is a glorious reading[3]
On a preserved tablet."
– Sura 56, verses 77 to 80:
"This is a glorious reading[3]

In a book well kept
Which none but the purified teach
This is a Revelation from the Lord of the Worlds."

– Sura 25, verse 5:
"They said: Tales of the ancients which he has caused to be written and they are dictated to him morning and evening."

Here we have a reference to the accusations made by the Prophet's enemies who treated him as an imposter. They spread the rumour that stories of antiquity were being dictated to him and he was writing them down or having them transcribed (the meaning of the word is debatable, but one must remember that Muhammad was illiterate). However this may be, the verse refers to this act of making a written record which is pointed out by Muhammad's enemies themselves.

A sura that came after Hegira makes one last mention of the leaves on which these divine instructions were written:

– Sura 98, verses 2 and 3:
"An (apostle) from God recites leaves
Kept pure where are decrees right and straight."

The Qur'an itself therefore provides indications as to the fact that it was set down in writing at the time of the Prophet. It is a known fact that there were several scribes in his following, the most famous of whom, Zaid Ibn Thābit, has left his name to posterity.

In the preface to his French translation of the Qur'an (1971), Professor Hamidullah gives an excellent description of the conditions that prevailed when the text of the Qur'an was written, lasting up until the time of the Prophet's death:

"The sources all agree in stating that whenever a fragment of the Qur'an was revealed, the Prophet called one of his literate companions and dictated it to him, indicating at the same time the exact position of the new fragment in the fabric of what had already been received . . . Descriptions note that Muhammad asked the scribe to reread to him what had been dictated so that he could correct any deficiencies . . . Another famous story tells how every year in the month of Ramadan, the Prophet would recite the whole of the Qur'an (so far revealed) to Gabriel . . . , that in the Ramadan preceding Muhammad's death, Gabriel had made him recite it twice . . . It is known how since the Prophet's time, Muslims acquired the habit of keeping vigil during Ramadan, and of reciting the whole of the Qur'an in addition to the usual prayers expected of them. Several sources add that Muhammad's scribe Zaid was present at this final bringing-together of the texts. Elsewhere, numerous other personalities are mentioned as well."

Extremely diverse materials were used for this first record: parchment, leather, wooden tablets, camels' scapula, soft stone for inscriptions, etc.

At the same time however, Muhammad recommended that the faithful learn the Qur'an by heart. They did this for a part if not all of the text recited during prayers. Thus there were *Ḥafiẓūn* who knew the whole of the Qur'an by heart and spread it abroad. The method of doubly preserving the text both in writing and by memorization proved to be extremely precious.

Not long after the Prophet's death (632), his successor Abu Bakr, the first Caliph of Islam, asked Muhammad's former head scribe, Zaid Ibn Thābit, to make a copy; this he did. On Omar's initiative (the future second Caliph), Zaid consulted all the information he could assemble at Madina: the witness of the *Ḥafiẓūn,* copies of the Book written on various materials belonging to private individuals, all with the object of avoiding possible errors in transcription. Thus an extremely faithful copy of the Book was obtained.

The sources tell us that Caliph Omar, Abu Bakr's successor in 634, subsequently made a single volume *(muṣḥaf)* that he preserved and gave on his death to his daughter Hafsa, the Prophet's widow.

The third Caliph of Islam, Uthman, who held the caliphate from 644 to 655, entrusted a commission of experts with the preparation of the great recension that bears his name. It checked the authenticity of the document produced under Abu Bakr which had remained in Hafsa's possession until that time. The commission consulted Muslims who knew the text by heart. The critical analysis of the authenticity of the text was carried out very rigorously. The agreement of the witnesses was deemed necessary before the slightest verse containing debatable material was retained. It is indeed known how some verses of the Qur'an correct others in the case of prescriptions: this may be readily explained when one remembers that the Prophet's period of apostolic activity stretched over twenty years (in round figures). The result is a text containing an order of suras that reflects the order followed by the Prophet in his complete recital of the Qur'an during Ramadan, as mentioned above.

One might perhaps ponder the motives that led the first three Caliphs, especially Uthman, to commission collections and recensions of the text. The reasons are in fact very simple: Islam's expansion in the very first decades following Muhammad's death was very rapid indeed and it happened among peoples whose native language was not Arabic. It was absolutely necessary to ensure the spread of a text that retained its original purity: Uthman's recension had this as its objective.

Uthman sent copies of the text of the recension to the centres of the Islamic Empire and that is why, according to Professor Hamidullah, copies attributed to Uthman exist in Tashkent and Istanbul. Apart from one or two possible mistakes in copying, the oldest documents known to the present day, that are to be found throughout the Islamic world, are identical; the same is true for documents preserved in Europe (there are fragments in the Bibliothèque Nationale in Paris which, according to the experts, date from the Eighth and Ninth centuries A.D., i.e. the Second and Third Hegirian centuries). The numerous ancient texts that are known to be in existence all agree except for very minor variations which do not change the general meaning of the text at all. If the context sometimes allows more than one interpretation, it may well have to do with the fact that ancient writing was simpler than that of the present day.[4]

The 114 suras were arranged in decreasing order of length; there were nevertheless exceptions. The chronological sequence of the Revelation was not followed. In the majority of cases however, this sequence is known. A large number of descriptions are mentioned at several points in the text, sometimes giving rise to repetitions. Very frequently a passage will add details to a description that appears elsewhere in an incomplete form. Everything connected with modern science is, like many subjects dealt with in the Qur'an, scattered throughout the book without any semblance of classification.

Notes and References

1. Muhammad's departure from Makka to Madina, 622 A.D.

2. Muhammad was totally overwhelmed by these words. We shall return to an interpretation of them, especially with regard to the fact that Muhammad could neither read nor write.

3. In the text: *Qur'ān* which also means 'reading'.

4. The absence of diacritical marks, for example, could make a verb either active or passive and in some instances, masculine or feminine. More often than not however, this was hardly of any great consequence since the context indicated the meaning in many instances.

Appendix 3

On Being Muslim: The Faith Dimension of Muslim Identity*

By
Willem A. Bijlefeld

People should not live by *bread* alone – and neither persons nor nations should be described and interpreted in terms of *faith* alone.[1] Probably the most serious injustice done to Islam by the Western press in recent years has been the tendency to use the word *Islam* as the magic key to unlocking the doors behind which all so-called mysteries of the Muslim world are hidden, to see Islam as the single or at least the foremost category for explaining all that is happening in Muslim nations.[2] There is no need to dwell on the irony of the fact that a religious and cultural tradition so little known in the West as Islam is, provided in 1978–79 one of the key words for the headlines of countless articles dealing with events susceptible to entirely different interpretations than the 'religious' one: "Passions and Perils: An Anxious Washington Studies the Fever in Islam," "Islam in Ferment," "The Islam Explosion," "Islamic Fanaticism Threatens World Security," "Islam Militant."[3] More recently V.S. Naipaul attracted the attention of many by the record of his visit to Iran, Pakistan, Malaysia, and Indonesia. While *Among the Believers* claims that it seeks to describe the human and political condition of these countries where Islam is significantly present,[4] the book is radically at odds with what Edward Said formulated as the necessity to take seriously "the human dimension of Islam," with honest "respect for the concrete detail of human experience,"

*Yvonne Haddad, *The Islamic Impact* (Syracuse: Syracuse University Press, 1984), pp. 219–39. By permission of the publisher.

avoiding "limiting labels like 'the Islamic mind' or 'the Islamic personality.' "[5] Said's concern is that as a rule Western coverage of events in the Muslim world has almost consistently failed to discriminate between "religious passion, a struggle for a just cause, ordinary human weakness, political competition, and the history of men, women, and societies seen *as* the history of men, women, and societies."[6] Where Said is questioning "how really useful . . . 'Islam' [is] as a concept for understanding Morocco *and* Saudi Arabia *and* Syria *and* Indonesia,"[7] Naipaul presents his visit to four Muslim nations as "An *Islamic* Journey" – the subtitle of the book that concludes with a section entitled "*Islamic* Winter," containing reflections on his second visit to Tehran in February 1981.[8]

Two interrelated issues are at stake. It is *at best* a modest step forward when one moves from a discussion of Islam as if it were a monolithic entity and a closed religious or philosophical system to a consideration of 900 million people[9] in this world simply in terms of their being "believers," Muslims. Islam is undoubtedly an extremely important dimension of the life of individual Muslims and Muslim societies, and the common Muslim insistence on the character of Islam as an all-encompassing way of life should not be taken lightly. But this does not mean that the complex reality of individual lives, national situations, and international relations anywhere in the Muslim world can be interpreted solely by a reference to Islam, only "Islamically." As a correlate to this, it is obviously inadequate to seek to define what Islam is and what being a Muslim implies primarily or even exclusively on the basis of observations of the actual behaviour of a group – even a relatively large group – of Muslims and a study of the current condition in various Muslim societies. The observer's perspective is clearly recognizable in, for example, a description of Pakistan as "the land of faith turning into a land of plunder," and in the reminiscence of Indonesia as the land where "people floated. Whether they moved forward, into a new civilization, or backward . . . towards the purer Arab faith, they were now always entering somebody else's world, and getting further from themselves."[10] But even the most accurate description of a Muslim community does not necessarily reflect what Islam can and does mean to many Muslims. In all religious traditions and communities there are persons and events that obscure rather than reflect what many of those who live in it see as the true character of their faith. Muhammad Abduh certainly does not stand alone in his observation that "Islam is concealed from western people by a heavy curtain of Muslims," and he shares with many the awareness of the need to distinguish between the true character of the religion of Islam and "those Muslims who by their conduct have been an argument against it."[11]

That obviously creates a predicament. "A heavy curtain of Muslims" may block our vision of what Islam really is – but on the other hand we do not want to deal with Islam as an abstraction, ignoring the concreteness of Muslims' way of life and conduct, their hopes and fears, aspirations and frustrations. We are aware of the immense variety and the ever-changing scenes in the Muslim world – regionally, culturally, politically, economically, and above all humanly. Almost blinded by the splendor of this diversity, we need to discover the common elements, that which is permanent, abiding, and distinctively "Islamic." We know that "being Muslim" implies much more than the acceptance of a particular set of beliefs, and the question of identity is for most Muslims infinitely more than a matter of private introspection.[12] Rafiuddin Ahmed provides us in his study *The Bengal Muslims 1871–1906* with an excellent example of the social, cultural, linguistic, and political ramifications of the issue of an identity crisis at a communal level.[13] Certainly in the case of the Muslim world we cannot draw sharp dividing lines between individual and communal experience, between the "spiritual" and the "material," between religion and politics, economics and arts. For any religious tradition, most definitely the Muslim, the word "faith" is misused unless it refers to a lived reality and real persons.[14] It is impossible in this introductory essay to do justice to this fully human character of faith, in this case faith as experienced and lived by those among us who are Muslims. But in restricting ourselves to the modest task of delineating some of the major themes of the Quran, we are not allowed to forget that we deal with commitments that continue to shape the lives of hundreds of millions of people.

We need to raise explicitly the question which unavoidably arises whenever an "outsider" speaks on – and to some extent, for – Islam: does a person who is not a Muslim have the mental ability and the moral right to seek to answer the question what it means to be a Muslim? The response that all that we do is simply to pass on what Muslims think and say about the subject is, understandably, far from convincing for those who raise the question, and, to say the least, irresponsibly naive. Any anthology of Muslim sayings and writings, growing out of the conviction that "the basic tenets of Islam come alive most simply in what Muslims themselves say,"[15] represents necessarily a personal choice and is a far from simple exercise.[16] Moreover, as anthologies grow larger and selections more varied, a coherent picture of what those basic tenets are becomes increasingly difficult to obtain. It does not seem appropriate to seek to protect ourselves against the accusation of a biased selectivity by simply taking shelter in the safety of a mere repetition of time-honored Muslim creedal statements or a survey of the traditional six points of the Muslim faith, and even the choice of Quranic themes and the interpretation suggested is, admittedly, a personal, subjective decision.

The legitimacy of people speaking for a religious tradition other than their own, first raised mainly as a more or less rhetorical question by some Western historians of religions, has now become, in many circles, a rather tense issue in inter-religious relationships. Many persons who year after year feel free to interpret and represent the basic tenets of a tradition other than their own turn out to be extremely sensitive, impatient, and defensive as soon as someone from the other community begins to participate in the process of trying to articulate what faith means and implies in *their* tradition. Mutuality is a painful process for many persons claiming to be interested in inter-religious conversations.

While we need to remain constantly aware of the risk – especially the *moral* risk – involved in any attempt at cross-religious interpretation, we also need to realize that to shun that risk means to give in to the dangerous claims of a religious absolutism and a theological exclusivism that ultimately denies the possibility of cross-cultural and inter-religious understanding, and, most importantly, forgets that in the final analysis there can be no outsiders to "faith" if faith is a matter of being truly human.[17] Therefore we proceed and, confronted with an endless variety of data interpreted and ordered by Muslims throughout the centuries in a great variety of ways, we accept the risks of selectivity and of subjective emphases and interpretations. Embarking upon such an adventure is a pretentious imposition unless one is prepared to submit "again and again to correction by the facts"[18] – first among those facts being the reactions of those who participate in the tradition we seek to understand – a principle far more clearly articulated than implemented by many historians and phenomenologists of religion. What follows can, therefore, lay no claim to objectivity, and lacks, one might say, the authenticity of the participant's perspective. Its justification lies elsewhere. Hans Küng stated that his book *On Being a Christian* "was written, not because the author thinks he is a good Christian, but because he thinks that being a Christian is a particularly good thing."[19] In a somewhat similar manner, the following account of the faith dimension of Muslim identity is offered not because the author can claim to be a good Muslim but because he is convinced that it is a particularly good thing for all of us to begin to understand and appreciate something of what "being a Muslim" implies. Moreover, there remains the question of whether the distinction between "theirs" and "ours" is valid when we talk about faith. For if faith is the ultimate dimension of human existence, the recognition of the singular should not be jeopardized by whatever can be said about the specifics of how it is articulated in various religious traditions.

Four closely related themes will be dealt with: (1) the twofold insistence on the universal and the particular; (2) progress without innovation; (3) the balanced middle: the power of the double affirmation; and (4) the unity of God and the wholeness of *Islam*.

The Twofold Emphasis on the Universal and the Particular

One of the most common themes in recent Muslim literature all over the world is that of the universality of Islam, grounded in its recognition of the One God, infinite in majesty and mercy, Lord of the Worlds. While the frequency of the expression of this notion in our time is remarkable, all the elements of this confession can be traced back to the Quran itself, and all of them have been part and parcel of Muslim faith and thought throughout the centuries: the unity of God – the unity of the universe and the original unity of humankind (S. 2:213 and 10:19; cf. 11:118) –

the unity of revelation and the oneness of religion. For our present purposes, two points seem of special importance:

1. The notion of universality is frequently elaborated in terms of a theological inclusivism as far as (particularly) the Jews and the Christians are concerned. President Sadat's speech to the Israeli Knesset in November 1977[20] and a large number of public exchanges of expressions of goodwill between Muslims and Christians have drawn the attention of many to Quranic verses stressing the bond between Jews, Christians, and Muslims, especially the unambiguous affirmation "We believe in God and in what has been revealed to us and what was revealed to Abraham, Ishmael, Isaac, Jacob, and the tribes, and that which Moses and Jesus received, and that what the Prophets received from their Lord" (S. 2:136 and 3:84) and the solemn declaration "We believe in that which has been revealed unto us and revealed unto you: our God and your God is One, and unto Him we unreservedly commit ourselves" (S. 29:46).[21] More than thirty texts in the Quran deal directly with this issue of a recognition of earlier revelations – it is the Same God, the Only One, who is the source of all of them, not infrequently in the context of an appeal to Christians to recognize the Quran on the basis of what they themselves have received.[22] While these data are often interpreted in an exclusivistic sense,[23] sometimes the emphasis is on the positive value of different religions and communities and the necessity to recognize the Muslim community "as *a* community among communities."[24]

2. In the two-fold Muslim emphasis on the universal and the particular, an important point to note is the theological order of the two and, related to it, the issue that *particularity* in Islam is definitely not ethnic or religious *particularism*. The celebration of the revelation of the Quran, "noble," "glorious" and "wonderful," (S. 56:77; 50:1; 85:21; 72:1) a Scripture "in clear Arabic language" (S. 26:195; 16:10)[25] is placed in the context of the recognition of earlier revelation. With a slightly different emphasis than Kenneth Cragg places in his statement that "there was continuity in the Scriptural idea and discontinuity in its final incidence,"[26] I would suggest "inseparable continuity and definitive culmination" as a way to summarize the Quranic view of the interrelatedness of all revealed Scriptures.

While the New Testament order is from Jerusalem to the ends

of the earth, Islam – or perhaps, rather, the Quran – starts with "the worlds" and then moves to the events around Mecca and Medina. The Quran never even hints at "a God of the Arabs" who is later on confessed to be the Lord of the Worlds: it starts with the Lord of the Worlds who *now* has also spoken to the Arabs.[27] Islam does not begin with a celebration of the revelatory event of the Quran and then proceeds to reflect on the possibility of revelation also outside the Quranic realm; it *starts* with the recognition of previous revelation and then celebrates that at last those who were without Scripture have also been included among "the People of the Book," that at last they too have become partakers of the blessings of Abraham's family – Prophethood, Scripture, and Wisdom.[28]

The wording chosen obviously intends to highlight important structural differences with at least major trends in the Hebrew Scriptures and the New Testament and the historical development of Jewish and Christian thought. There is no opportunity to go more carefully and precisely into this comparison. But the very idioms of our Scriptures show remarkable variances on this point. The Quran, e.g., does not use one single time the expression "the God of Abraham" or "the God of our Fathers" (let alone, as stated before, "the God of the Arabs"). The significant notion of the religion of Abraham denotes Abraham as the archetype of the true believer, rather than in any way limiting God to a covenant relation with a segment of the human population. Words for "covenant" and "election" occur in the Quran, but they have a content and emphasis significantly different from that in the Hebrew Scriptures,[29] and so one could continue with a series of interrelated issues. Thinking of Moubarac's provocative statement that we find in the Quran "a history of religion rather than a religion of history,"[30] one wonders whether – without exaggerating the distinction between the two notions as if they were radically exclusive of each other – one would be justified in suggesting that the Quran is concerned with the revelatory dimension of the histories of nations[31] rather than with revelation as history. "Islam did not arise out of the history of a covenant with God, as in the case with Judaism. An intimate connexion between God and man based on interaction in history is unknown to Islam," Smail Balic wrote.[32]

Progress Without Innovation

Many daily and weekly papers in the U.S.A. have in the past few years published articles on the issue of "Islam and Modernization." With some regularity reference is made to widespread Muslim distrust of any "innovation." Innovations, whether they are heretical teachings or new patterns of behavior, are often seen, we are told, as dangerously undermining the unity, solidarity, and homogeneity of the community of the faithful. While generalizations are as meaningless here as in the description of any other aspect of current conditions in the Muslim world, one cannot deny that the word *innovation* has negative connotations for a large number of Muslims.

In this connection, and not unrelated to the issue discussed in the preceding section, one Quranic verse seems of special relevance S. 46:9, where the Prophet is instructed by God: "Say: I am not an innovation among the Messengers," "not an innovator," "no bringer of new-fangled doctrines," "no new thing."[33] This emphasis on the continuity of revelation has led people to raise the question whether the Quran contains the notion of a progressive revelation. The question has been answered positively and negatively, by Muslims as well as others, and the answer given determines or reflects the author's view of the relation between Islam and other religions. Whenever the discussion focuses on the unity of revelation and the recognition of previous Scriptures, the tendency is to stress that all God's messengers came with basically the same message.[34] Whenever an appeal is made by Muslims to other "people of the Book" to move from partial knowledge to an acceptance of and belief in all of the Book,[35] including the Quran, the uncorrupted embodiment of the Revelation, the emphasis is almost bound to be on the notion of a progressive revelation, frequently spelled out in terms of various "stages" in the history of revelation corresponding to different levels of receptivity and comprehension.[36]

A Quranic expression often used to substantiate the thesis that all of God's messengers stand, as it were, on the same level, undifferentiated, is the declaration – in a rather common translation – that "we make no distinction between any of them." In the light of S. 4:150 and 152 the expression referred to should be interpreted not as a denial of different ranks but as an urgent warning that we should not discriminate against any of God's apostles, that is, we should not recognize some while refusing to acknowledge others.[37] That seems a point of major significance for any attempt to understand the Islamic view of other religions. In Muslim perspective a refusal by Christians to acknowledge Muhammad and the Quran is inconsistent with their acceptance of Jesus and the Gospel, in the same manner that a Jewish refusal to recognize Jesus is seen as inconsistent with their acknowledgement of Moses and the Taurat. It is, therefore, this particular notion of inclusivism that has given rise to some of the most bitter polemics between Jews, Christians, and Muslims. The Muslims' deep-rooted conviction of the unity of God's revelation fills many of them with honest amazement and even bewilderment as to why a Christian whose sincerity they do not challenge can possibly be so blinded as not to be willing to include the event of the Quran in his or her own faith perspective. "Discontinuity" is thus seen not as brought about by, and in, the sending down of the Quran, but by human arrogance that leads people to an ungrateful denial of some of God's messengers and their message; *they* are seen as being guilty of "exclusivism."

If we want to use the term progress in connection with Quranic perspectives on the history of revelations, it is definitely not *primarily* a matter of ever new insights and truths being added[38] – there is no innovation – but rather one of a definitive safeguarding of the revelation against corruption and distortion, an assurance most strongly expressed in the Quranic statement that God Himself stands guard over the Quran (S. 15:9).

There is unmistakably the tendency among many Muslims to emphasize the "permanence" of the truth of the Quran, a permanence not challenged, in their view, by the necessity to relate their understanding of the Quranic message to ever-changing conditions.[39] "Islam does not need to be modernized. Islam has always been modern," wrote a leader of the World Muslim Congress some years ago.[40] Such a statement reflects, no doubt, the conviction of the "contemporaneity" of the Quran for every new generation. But it may also be related to the wider notion of the unity and continuity of all revelation: no revelation can become outdated because revelation is ultimately ahistorical. A statement by a contemporary Muslim provides a helpful illustration of this point of view that has far-reaching consequences for many of the issues in our time: "[divine guidance] . . . remains or should remain forever unaltered by time or history . . . There is no reason to conceive of revelation as something temporal or historical."[41]

**The Balanced Middle,
The Power of the Double Affirmation**

Although it occurs only once in the Quran, S. 2:143, the designation of the Muslim community as "a middle nation" (Pickthall) plays a significant role in many Muslim descriptions and interpretations of their tradition – "An *Ummat* justly balanced," Abdullah Yusuf Ali renders it, while Fazlur Rahman opts for "Median community."[42] Although made in a different context, Fazlur Rahman's remark on the Quranic notion of the "middle road" seems to articulate what several Muslims sense to be the characteristically Islamic vision: "the mean of the Quran" is not "a negative mean . . . from which both sides are absent," but rather "a positive, creative mean, an integrative moral organism," "the unique balance of integrative moral action."[43] Many of those who hear in this expression primarily a warning to shun excesses often work out the ethical implications as a rejection of the Christian ideal of self-denial on the one side and a denial of cruel self-assertion on the other, while on the popular-political level it is not uncommon to find this designation used in the discussion of the place of the Arab or the Muslim world as a third way in between the blocks of communism and capitalism.[44]

In whatever context it occurs, there is undoubtedly for many a powerful appeal in this refusal to accept a number of alternatives as mutually exclusive options, and rather to affirm both and to find the characteristic Muslim position in the balanced synthesis. A few illustrations of such double affirmations must suffice.[45]

Returning once more to the issue of the relation between the Quran and earlier revelations, a widely accepted Muslim interpretation – attracting already the attention of a seventeenth-century Western Christian student of the Quran[46] – is that the "newness" of the Quran does not lie in any new truths but in the affirmation and integration of what were one-sided emphases in the (interpretation of) the Book of Moses and the Gospel of

Jesus. The message of justice in the Taurat (Divine justice as well as justice and retaliation in society) became integrated with Jesus' proclamation of love and forgiveness, the latter as one-sided in the Christian context as justice was in the Old Testament. The Old Testament understanding of the function of religion and its vision of the necessity to bring all of life under the guidance of the Law was joined with the Christian emphasis on the need for a personal response to God's acts of grace and its constant reminder of the reality of the world to come.

S. 5:48, e.g., seems indeed to suggest such a process of integration and "balancing": "And therein We prescribed for them 'A life for a life, an eye for an eye, a nose for a nose, an ear for an ear, a tooth for a tooth, and for wounds retaliation.' But whosoever foregoes it as a freewill offering, that shall be for him an expiation" (Arberry's translation). Whatever the difficulties in translation and interpretation are, the basic meaning is clear: retaliation is not ruled out – an eye for any eye has still its validity – but the option for a voluntary charity, a remission of the retaliation, is always there.

Far more pronounced in the Quranic proclamation is the other double affirmation mentioned already: that of this life *and* the next. The Islamic concern with this-worldly affairs has received a one-sided emphasis lately in many superficial or seriously distorted descriptions of the phenomenon of Islamic resurgence. The relevance and significance of one of the major issues at stake, namely the role of religion in and for society, can perhaps most easily be illustrated by a reference to Fazlur Rahman's article "Islam: Challenges and Opportunities."[47] Noting "the multiple phenomena of lawlessness and chaos" in Western society and observing that "Western civilization is a giant now fully corroded from within," Fazlur Rahman suggests a crucial distinction between Islam and Christianity, the latter now weakened "even as a spiritual force," but in a sense traditionally inadequate in as far as it "almost never oriented either the polity or the other social institutions of the Christian peoples, except for marriage. Islam, on the other hand, has had, as its central task – and this is its very genesis – to construct a social order on a very ethical basis. In the execution of this task, its very spirituality, that is, a genuine morality, is at work: it is asceticism *in* this world."[48] While "at the moment . . . the Muslim community is not prepared to play this role . . . and does not know how to recover and reconstruct Islam," Islam has a tremendously important role in and for the world at large: "For the world, at this critical juncture of its history, appears to offer a unique opportunity for Islam to play its due role in the construction of a viable future for humanity."[49]

A description of Islam as critically concerned with the order of *this* world needs to be complemented, as indicated above, by a reference to the Quranic reminder of the transitory nature of "the enjoyment of the life of the world" (S. 42:36; cf. S. 40:39; 10:24; 18:45–6; 87:16–17), its admonition that "the life of the world is only play, and idle talk, and pageantry, and boasting among you, and rivalry in respect of wealth and children" (S. 57:20). "This life of the world is but a pastime and a game. Lo – the Home of the Hereafter: *that* is Life" (S. 29:64; cf. S. 6:32; 47:36). "The life of this world is but comfort of illusion" (S. 3:185; cf. S. 46:20).

The notion of "asceticism *in* this world" is not unrelated to this awareness of the world to come and our human accountability to God: when "hell will be set afire, and paradise brought nigh, a soul will know what it has earned" (S. 81:12–14) – a theme recurring most frequently in the earlier suras of the Quran but definitely present in late Medinan suras as well.[50]

"Revelation *and* Reason" is another double affirmation often emphasized,[51] not entirely unrelated to the view of both history *and* nature as equally important realms of revelation and the understanding of Islam as both the final and the primal religion.[52] That in a Muslim catechism with a question and answer format[53] each question receives a double answer, the first one based on reason, the second one on Quranic texts, would normally not be seen as a "compromise" in the negative sense, since many Muslims would challenge the thesis that there exists "always and in all religions a relationship of distrust between revelation and reason."[54]

The Unity of God and the "Wholeness" of Islam

Especially in past centuries several "outsiders" have suggested that there is a major inconsistency in what these observers interpreted as the most characteristic "double affirmation" of Islam:

its fundamental testimony to "God *and* Muhammad." We need to begin to grasp the crucial significance of "that eloquent 'and' that links the Unity of God with the Apostleship of Muhammad,"[55] while doing justice to the persistent Muslim insistence that Islam is absolutely uncompromising in its affirmation of the Unity of God – the One to Whom "none is equal" (S. 112:4),[56] who does not share His power and majesty with anyone (S. 17:111; 18:26; 25:2; 27:60–1) who has no "associates" and no "offspring."[57] Only in passing can we refer to the tragic distortion of the reality of the faith of Muslims by those who in the past insinuated that the radical monotheism of Islam reduces the confession of the Oneness of God to the level of arithmetics. At stake and implied in the witness that "there is no God but He"[58] are, among many other notions, the richly diverse elements of the recognition of His majesty and power, the affirmation of His sovereign freedom,[59] the celebration of His being "our sufficiency" (S. 65:3; 3:173; 8:64; cf. S. 39:36), the assurance of His self-commitment to mercy (S. 6:12, 54),[60] and the awareness of our total dependency on Him.

The confession that there is "none besides Him" is, in Muslim perspective, in no way compromised by the "and" of "God and His messenger," but receives its ultimate foundation in the second part of the Muslim affirmation of faith; for it is exactly in and through the revelation of the Quran and the prophethood of Muhammad that the testimony to the Oneness and Unity of God is brought to its utmost clarity and defended against all kinds of distortions.

One can hardly overstate the powerful impact which the Prophet has on the daily lives of Muslims,[61] the significance of his exemplary role, the earnestness of the devotion which remembers him, in short, of the continuing desire to "celebrate" him.[62] Ignoring or downplaying this aspect of Islam is as much of a distortion of the Muslim tradition as interpreting it as being inconsistent with the first part of the Islamic witness.

Exactly because God is One, the response to Him needs to be "undivided." The Arabic word "islam" expresses in a most succinct manner the interrelatedness of the recognition of the Oneness of God and the totality of the commitment it requires. The archetype of this proper response to God is Abraham. He approached his Lord "with an undivided heart," and he and his son "submitted" when God tested them – using two interrelated expressions of the Abraham narrative in S. 37:84 and 103 (cf. S. 2:131).

In this unquestioning commitment to God the elements of obedience and humility clearly play an important role. But there are other aspects as well, among them especially a sense of security, peace, tranquility, confidence and assurance,[63] and very importantly the element of gratitude.[64] As the signs of God's power and majesty in this world are as clear as "the imprints of His mercy" (S. 30:50), so awe and gratitude are interrelated in the human response.

This total commitment is possible only because there is none besides God worthy to be worshipped and obeyed. As there is "none besides Him," so there is no realm of life unrelated to Islam as a response to Him. Whatever in any given situation the need may be for differentiating between roles and functions of people within the community of believers and in the society at large, Islam cannot be reduced to the kind of creedal affirmation that would forget to ponder and give thanks for the most diverse signs of God's active involvement in all of life. S. 30 lists the rest found in the relationship between spouses, the plurality of languages and colours, the quickening rain after a dry spell, and "herald winds that give you a taste of His mercy" as "signs" alongside that of the sending of His messengers (verses 20, 21, 22, 23, 24, 25, 46).[65]

Abu Hurayra's report on something the Prophet used to say seems to summarize much of what has been said and to hint at much more that has been left unspoken:

> O Lord of Everything
> O Sender down of the Law, the Gospels and the Quran . . .
> Thou art the First and there was nothing before Thee
> Thou art the Last and there is nothing after Thee
> and Thou dost hide Thyself and there is nothing
> beyond Thee.[66]

Notes

1. "Faith is a quality of the whole person. It has, therefore, as many dimensions as has personhood," W. Cantwell Smith wrote, *Faith and Belief* (Princeton, N.J.: Princeton University Press, 1979), p. 158. In the following article the word *faith* is not used in as sharp a distinction from the *belief* as Smith wants to maintain, but in full awareness of the fact that "faith is a response to what one indisputably knows to be of divine origin," Wilfred Cantwell Smith, "Faith as *Taṣdīq*," in *Islamic Philosophical Theology,* ed. Parviz Morewedge (Albany: State University of New York Press, 1979), p. 113. For a recent discussion of Smith's position see Donald Wiebe, "The Role of 'Belief' in the Study of Religion. A Response to W. C. Smith," *Numen* 26 (1979): 234–49 and Wilfred Cantwell Smith, "Belief: A Reply to a Response," *Numen* 27 (1980): 247–55.

2. This point is emphasized strongly by Edward W. Said, *Covering Islam: How the Media and the Experts Determine How We See the Rest of the World* (New York: Pantheon Books, 1981). See below notes 5, 6, and esp. 7.

3. These titles have been selected arbitrarily from a long list of headlines of articles dealing primarily with political, social, and economic events and developments in Muslim parts of the world, but all of them using the word "Islam" in the title. The articles here mentioned appeared in *New York Times,* Dec. 9, 1979; *U.S. News and World Report,* Dec. 10, 1979; *New Republic,* Dec. 8, 1979; *Journal Inquirer,* Nov. 30, 1979; *Christian Science Monitor,* Dec. 14, 1978, respectively.

4. V. S. Naipaul, *Among the Believers: An Islamic Journey* (New York: Alfred A. Knopf, 1981).

5. Said, *Covering Islam,* pp. xxxi, 152.

6. Ibid., p. 7.

7. Ibid., p. xv; see also p. xix (". . . I do not believe as strongly and as firmly in the notion of 'Islam' as many experts, policymakers, and general intellectuals do; on the contrary, I often think it has been more of a hindrance than a help in understanding what moves people and societies") and pp. 38, 53, 56–60, 77ff.

8. Naipaul, *Among the Believers,* pp. 401–30.

9. Estimates of the world total of Muslims continue to vary widely, from the consistently low figures in the *Encyclopaedia Britannica* (the *1982 Book of the Year* estimate is 592,157,900) to the high of more than one billion given in many Muslim sources. Of interest are the data in the *World Christian Encyclopedia,* ed. David B. Barrett (Nairobi: Oxford University Press, 1982), p. 6. While his figures for the present are much lower than commonly estimated, he anticipates an increase of almost 95,000,000 between 1980 and 1985 and of more than 477 million between 1980 and the year 2000.

10. Naipaul, *Among the Believers,* pp. 86 and 305 respectively.

11. The first quotation is found in Charis Wady, *The Muslim Mind* (London: Longmans, 1976), p. xvii (from a letter from Dr. Hassan Hathout), the second quote is from Muhammad Abduh, *The Theology of Unity (Risālat al-Tawḥīd),* trans. Ishaq Musaad and Kenneth Cragg (London: George Allen and Unwin, 1965), p. 154.

12. Nadav Safran rightly observed in his review of Anwar el-Sadat's *In Search of Identity* (New York: Harper and Row, 1978) that Mr. Sadat meant by it "the search for a practical philosophy of life and guiding ideals and goals, rather than a narrow psychological sense of one's self"; *New York Times Book Review,* May 7, 1978.

13. Rafiuddin Ahmed, *The Bengal Muslims, 1871–1906. A Quest for Identity.* (Delhi: Oxford University Press, 1981), esp. Ch. IV: "A Crisis of Identity: Muslims or Bengalis?"

14. See Wilfred Cantwell Smith, *Faith and Belief,* pp. 48–49: "Faith, in Islamic theology, was set forth as first a personal relationship to truth *(tasdiq):* a recognizing of it, appropriating it to one's self, and resolving to live in accord with it."

15. Wady, *The Muslim Mind,* p. xvi.

16. The critical issue is not, using Khurram Murad's words, that "an anthology selects, necessarily, only what the selector's eye discerns as suitable, and only in such measure and such arrangement as he judges to be appropriate" – Khurram Murad, in a review of Kenneth Cragg and R. Marston Speight, *Islam from Within: Anthology of a Religion* (Belmont, Calif.: Wadsworth, 1980), in *The Muslim World Book Review* 2, no. 1 (Spring 1982): 5. Nor is it that "the anthologist's own understanding, preferences, priorities, even inner dispositions" are reflected in his choice of material. The crucial question is whether anyone attempting a "descriptive" introduction to a religious tradition – either in the form of an anthology or in some brief observations as offered here – is critically aware of those preferences and priorities, and at least indirectly deals with the criteria for what is considered "suitable" and "appropriate" by stating openly the objective of his presentation.

17. "The locus of faith is persons" Wilfred Cantwell Smith insists; *Faith and Belief,* p. 158. But in seeing faith as "the prodigious hallmark of being human" (p. 142), Smith in no way denies its transcending dimension: "Faith is that quality of or available to humankind by which we are characterized as transcending, or are enabled to transcend, the natural order – an order both in and beyond which, simultaneously, it has been normal, we may observe, for men and women to live."

18. G. van der Leeuw, *Religion in Essence and Manifestation* (Gloucester, Mass: Peter Smith, 1967), p. 685.

19. Hans Küng, *On Being A Christian* (Garden City, N.J.: Doubleday, 1976), pp. 20–21.

20. The English translation is included in el-Sadat, *In Search of Identity: An Autobiography,* pp. 330–43; the reference to S. 2:136 is in the concluding paragraph, p. 343.

21. Already in the twelfth century a Bishop of Sidon, Paul of Antioch, brought together the Quranic texts he considered as speaking in favour of Christ and the Christians, including the verse here mentioned as well as, among others, S. 5:82; 42: 15, 10:94; 3:55; 22:40 and texts dealing with the Quran "authenticating" previous Scriptures, those speaking highly of the Injil and of Christ and his Virgin Mother. See Paul Khoury, *Paul d'Antioche, Évêque melkite de Sidon (XIIe* S.) (Beirut: Impr. Catholique, n.d.), Arabic text pp. 59–83 (Arabic section), French trsl. pp. 169–87.

22. Most of these texts are enumerated in my "Some Recent Contributions to Qur'anic Studies, I" *MW* 64 (1974): 96.

23. Si Boubakeur Hamza, e.g., denies that there is a single Quranic text validating any non-Islamic beliefs *after* the revelation of the Quran: "Outside Islam there is no salvation." *Le Coran* (Paris: Fayard-Denoël, 1972), I, 32, 137, 237, 242, 247–48.

24. See especially Fazlur Rahman's comments on S. 5:48 in *Major Themes of the Qur'ān* (Minneapolis-Chicago: Bibliotheca Islamica, 1980), pp. 166–67. It occurs in an Appendix ("The People of the Book and Diversity of 'Religions' ") which appeared originally under the title "Christian Particularity and the Faith of Islam" in *Christian Faith in a Religiously Plural World,* ed. Donald G. Dawe and John B. Carman (Maryknoll, N.Y.: Orbis Books, 1978), pp. 69–79.

25. These and all other texts referring to the fact that this revelation was given in the Arabic language (S. 12:2; 20:113; 39:28; 41:3; 42:7; 43:3) occur in suras of the Meccan period and cannot be used as an argument on which to base the thesis that there was a development from a religious "Islamism" in Mecca to a nationalist, political "Arabism" in Medina, as Julian Obermann suggested in 1955; see for further references my "A Prophet and More Than A Prophet?" *MW* 59 (1969): 21, note 88.

26. Kenneth Cragg, *The Event of the Qur'ān* (London: George Allen and Unwin, 1971), p. 61.

27. Not in a "communal electionist" sense, as if God, after an earlier choice of other communities which then became disobedient, now has finally chosen the Arabs (see note 29 below), but rather with the emphasis on the tremendous responsibility now that God has spoken also to them through a messenger from among them, speaking their own language.

28. S. 29:27 speaks about "Prophethood and Scripture" having been established by God among the descendants of Abraham; S. 4:54 uses the language of "Scripture and Wisdom" having been bestowed upon Abraham's descendants; and S. 45:16 the three words, "Scripture, Wisdom and Prophethood" are combined, having been given to the children of Israel. Cf. also S. 3:79 (81) and 6:89. This is obviously not to deny that the Quran also affirms the

universality of God's revelation; "Every community has its messenger"; S. 10:47; 16:36; 17:15; 23:44; 30:47; cf. also S. 13:7 and 35:24.

29. Cf., e.g., Fazlur Rahman's remark that "the whole tenor of the Qur'ānic argument is against election" (with a reference to S. 2:124) and his observations on the Qur'ān's "strong rejection of exclusivism and election"; *Major Themes of the Qur'an*, pp. 165–66. The language of God "choosing" or "electing" is indeed very rare in the Quran, and never in the sense the word has in the Hebrew Scriptures. The verb *khara,* VIII, is used for Moses in S. 20:13, for the Children of Israel in 44:32, and in a general sense (whomever He wills) in 28:68. The verb *safa,* VIII, is used in connection with Noah, Adam, the family of Abraham, and the family of Imran in S. 3:33; Abraham, Isaac, and Jacob in 38:47; Abraham in 2:130; Moses in 7:144; Tabut (Saul) in 2:247; Mary in 3:42, and in a more general sense (His servants whom he has chosen) in 27:59 and 35:32.

30. Y. Moubarac, *Abraham dans le Coran* (Paris: J. Vrin, 1958), p. 139, note 2, with a reference to S. 3:17. On the same page the remark occurs that Islam "est une religion de la tradition plutôt que de l'histoire."

31. Used in the more general sense of groups of people, communities. A great number of Muslim writings speak about the immutable laws of God governing the rise and fall of civilizations and communities, their destruction due to their turning away from God's commandments, becoming oppressive, etc. A wide variety of such views and statements is discussed in Yvonne Yazbeck Haddad, *Contemporary Islam and the Challenge of History* (Albany: State University of New York Press, 1982); see, e.g., pp. 101, 105, 112–113 and 118 as well as the Appendices, esp. no. E ("Islam Looks at History" by Muhammad Kamal Ibrahim Jafar, pp. 174–80) and no. G ("The Qur'anic Interpretation of History" by Imad al-Din Khalil, pp. 188–204). One of the Quranic expressions relevant in this context is the challenge to travel over the earth and to see what the end was of those who gave the lie to the truth (S. 3:137; 6:11; 16:36) and to become wise by seeing what happened to those (sinners) who lived before (S. 12:109; 27:69; 30:9, 42; 35:44; 40:21, 82; 47:10).

32. "The Image of Jesus in Contemporary Islamic Theology," in *We Believe in One God,* ed. Annemarie Schimmel and Abdoljavad Falaturi (New York: The Seabury Press, 1979), p. 2.

33. In or according to the translations of A. J. Arberry [*The Koran Interpreted* (London: Oxford Univ. Press, 1964; first publ. 1955)], J. H. Kramers [*De Koran* (Amsterdam: Elsevier, 1956 and reprints); "Niet ben ik een nieuwlichter onder de boodschappers"], A. Yusuf Ali [*The Meaning of the Glorious Qur'ān* (Cairo-Beirut, n.d.; first publ. as *The Holy Qur'an,* 1934)], and Muhammad Marmaduke Pickthall [*The Meaning of the Glorious Qur'ān* (Mecca-New York: Muslim World League, 1977; first publ. 1930)] respectively. Muhammad Asad, allowing in a footnote for the translation here given as an alternative rendering, gives as his first choice: "I am not the first of [God's] apostles," basing this on the interpretation given by Tabari, Baghawi, Razi, and Ibn Kathir; *The Message of the Qur'ān* (Gibraltar: Dar al-Andalus, 1980).

34. See Fazlur Rahman's remark: "These messages are universal and identical": *Major Themes of the Qur'ān,* p. 163. An interesting qualification is given by Muhammad Asad in his footnotes to S. 46:9: "the Qur'anic doctrine of the identity of the *ethical* teachings propounded by all of God's prophets" (italics added).

35. The believers (Muslims) are addressed in S. 3:119 as "you who believe in all of the Book," in a passage dealing with the relation between them and "the People of the Book," Jews and Christians. Asad translates the beginning of vs. 119 as follows: "Lo! It is you who [are prepared to] love them, but they will not love you, although you believe in all of the revelation," and adds to these last words the footnote "i.e., including the revelation of the Bible." Whether one opts for that interpretation or – as seems preferable to me – reads with Arberry and others "you believe in the Book, all of it," the distinction remains between the true believers who accept all of God's revelation, including, particularly, its final embodiment, and those who refuse to acknowledge part of it.

36. The idea of a progressive revelation is, e.g., expressed by Mohammad Abd Allah Draz in his remark: "In the revelations of the Qur'an, as in every previous revelation, a new and original contribution is added to the earlier ones." "The Origin of Islam," in *Islam – The Straight Path,* ed. Kenneth W. Morgan (New York: Ronald Press, 1958), p. 34.

37. The expression referred to is found in S. 2:136, 285; 3:84. The idea of different "ranks" is found in S. 2:253. "We make no distinction between any of them," is the translation given in, among others, Pickthall, Muhammad Zafrulla Khan, *The Qur'an* (London, Dublin: Curzon Press, 1971; 3rd rev. ed. 1981), and Muhammad Asad. The last mentioned clarifies the meaning in his footnote to S. 2:136: "i.e., we regard them all as true prophets of God." Preferable, since it is less open to misunderstanding, is Arberry's: "We make no division between any of them." On the issue itself cf. Fazlur Rahman: "If Muḥammad and his followers believe in all prophets, all people must also and equally believe in him. Disbelief in him would be equivalent to disbelief in all, for this would arbitrarily upset the line of prophetic succession." *Major Themes of the Qur'ān,* p. 164.

38. The examples of a somewhat different emphasis given above do not render this observation invalid. Many Muslims emphasize as one of the distinctions that whereas all other prophets and messengers were sent to a particular "tribe," the Prophet Muhammad's role and function are for all of humankind.

39. The only issue raised with some frequency among Muslims is whether the notion of "immutability" also applies to some very specific legal commandments and prohibitions in the Quran. A few references can illustrate the variety of positions held. Ismail R. al-Faruqi, emphasizing that the Quran is "imperishable because God declared Himself its protector and guardian," speaks about the limited number of verses dealing with legislation (hardly 500 out of 6,342) as "of lesser importance than the rest," and sees this as a reason for the ongoing validity and applicability of the Quran: "They [Muslims] hold that God will not

need to send another revelation, partly because He has placed in human hands an imperishable and definitive statement of His will, that is the Qur'ān, and partly because He wishes people themselves to discover and to elaborate the means by which the will of God is henceforth to be realized. It is not by accident therefore that the Quranic revelation is not prescriptive in the main; it is because the divine plan relegated lawmaking to humankind, as long as the principles and values that the prescriptive laws embody are those which God has revealed" *Islam* (Niles, Ill.: Argus Comm., 1979), pp. 36–37. The need to distinguish clearly between "legal enactments" and "moral injunctions" is emphasized in many of Fazlur Rahman's writings. Rejecting the principle that "although a law is occasioned by a specific situation, its application nevertheless becomes universal," Fazlur Rahman maintains that it is exactly in order to do justice to the *ratio legis* – the "intention" of the law, the reason for its being enunciated – that specific laws have to be changed in changing circumstances: "When the situation so changes that the law fails to reflect the *ratio*, the law must change," *Major Themes of the Qur'ān*, pp. 47–49. A similar position is represented by Smail Balic, for example, in his article "Das Schari'a – Verständnis in pluralistischer Gesellschaft," *Islam und der Westen* 1, no. 1 (Jan. 1981): 2–3, where he stresses the need for a historical-critical study of the Quran ("Ein historisch-kritisches Qur'an – Verständnis stellt sich als unumgängliches Erfordernis ein") in order to be able to discover the meaning (purpose, intention) behind specific legal injunctions. In order to stress the fact that such an attempt is totally unacceptable to many (most) other Muslims, we conclude with the final sentence of Falaturi's article mentioned before. With reference to the discussions that took place at the conference in Freiburg, Germany in November 1974 he writes: "Muslims vigorously opposed any reference to an *historical* understanding of the Koran which might in any way put into question the existence of Islam and its laws as proclaimed by Muhammad," *We Believe in One God*, p. 73.

40. Inamullah Khan, "Islam in the Contemporary World," in *God and Man in Contemporary Islamic Thought*, ed. Charles Malik (Beirut: American University of Beirut, 1972), p. 12.

41. Falaturi, "Experience of Time and History in Islam," in *We Believe in One God*, p. 65.

42. F. Rahman, *Major Themes of the Qur'ān*, p. 145.

43. Ibid., p. 28.

44. "The essence of Islam is to avoid all extravagances on either side. It is a sober, practical religion," reads the beginning of the footnote Yusuf Ali has at S. 2:143. And in discussing Sayyid Qutb's view of the West and of the struggle between capitalism and communism, Yvonne Haddad writes, introducing a quotation from Sayyid Qutb: "There is no doubt that victory for Islam is assured because of its self-evident superiority and because Islam occupies what he calls the all-important middle position. Islam offers the world a balance that is 'not to be found in idealistic Christianity nor in dogmatic communism, but in a middle position about life. [Islam] as an ideology balances pure spirituality and moderate practical materialism and forms from them a system for the

conscience and a way of life, an everlasting vision for humanity.' " Y. Haddad, *Contemporary Islam,* p. 91. The quotation, in Haddad's translation, is from Qutb's *Nahwa Mujtama Islami* (Cairo, n.d.), p. 32.

45. See also, e.g., a passage in Anwar al-Jundi, *al-Islam wa Harakat al-Tarikh* (Cairo, 1968), p. 496, summarized as follows in Haddad, *Contemporary Islam,* p. 86: "Islam is the only system that provides for the coming together of body and spirit in man, of worship and works in life, of the world and the hereafter in religion, and of heaven and earth in the universe."

46. Dominicus Germanus (1588–1670) composed an "Interpretatio Alcoranus Literalis cum scholia," still unpublished, to which Sr. J. Marita Paul Colla is devoting a doctoral dissertation (forthcoming, Hartford). In the context of his discussion of the meaning of *al-Rahman* and *al-Rahim* – for which he accepts as the common Muslim interpretation that the words refer to God's grace in this world and the next – Dominicus quotes in Arabic and translates passages from Al-Kashani and others, and finally one from Ibn Kamal, describing the Jews as devoted to the worship of "external bodily pleasures and sensual appetite," the Christians as tending towards "the internal and the light of the World of holiness," while Muslims, truly worshipping the one God alone, are called to "rejoice in all things in this world and the next." Scholion on the Proemialis (Surat al-Fatiha).

47. *In Islam: Past Influence and Present Challenge* (in Honour of W. Montgomery Watt), ed. Alford T. Welch and Pierre Cachia (Edinburgh: Edinburgh University Press; Albany: State University of New York Press, 1979), pp. 315–30.

48. The references quoted are from *Islam: Past Influence,* pp. 328, 329, 330 respectively.

49. Ibid., p. 327.

50. One can hardly overemphasize the frequency and intensity of the Quranic admonition that in all actions all persons stand constantly under God's judgement, and its emphasis on ethical conduct. In elaborating this point, many Muslims stress the fact that the notion of "salvation," in the Christian sense, has no place in the Quran and in Islamic thought "For Islam, there is no particular 'salvation': there is only 'success *(falāh)*' or 'failure *(khusrān)*' in the task of building the type of [ethico-social] world order we are describing"; Fazlur Rahman, *Major Themes of the Qur'ān,* p. 63. For a few other examples of Muslim discussions of the notion of "salvation" see my "Other Faith Images of Jesus: Some Muslim Contributions to the Christological Discussion," in *Christological Perspectives,* ed. Robert F. Berkey and Sarah A. Edwards (New York: Pilgrim Press, 1982), p. 206 and p. 298, note 51.

51. For a general discussion of the relationship between revelation and reason in Islam see A. J. Arberry's *Revelation and Reason in Islam* (London: George Allen and Unwin, 1957). In several Muslim publications, also at the popular level, emphasis is laid upon the "rational" character of Islam, not infrequently with references to Muhammad Abduh-Rashid Rida's statement

about the complete harmony of the revelation God has granted in His uncreated Book, the Quran, and that found in His Created Word, Nature. In other Muslim expositions the emphasis is not so much on "reason" in a strictly intellectual sense, but rather on man's reasonableness, his conscience, his original orientation towards God, his inner disposition. Cf. S. 30:30 and the data in Jane I. Smith, *An Historical and Semantic Study of the Term Islam* (Missoula, Mont.: Scholars Press, 1975), pp. 123, 124, 193, 201. A very significant recent contribution to the discussion of the issue of intellect and revelation is Seyyed Hossein Nasr's *Knowledge and the Sacred* (New York: Crossroad, 1981). In the chapter "Scientia Sacra" (pp. 130–59) he writes (p. 148): "Although the Intellect shines within the being of man, man is too far removed from his primordial nature to be able to make full use of this divine gift by himself. He needs revelation which alone can actualize the intellect in man and allow it to function properly."

52. This double characterization of Islam as "final and primal religion," used in my "Islam's forstaelse af sig selv, I–II," *Nordisk Missions Tidsskrift* 74, no. 2 (1963): 37–46; no. 3 (1963): 25–37, became a widely accepted way of introducing Islam following Seyyed Hossein Nasr's elaboration of it in his *Ideals and Realities of Islam* (Boston: Beacon Press, 1972; originally published in 1966): "Islam, the last religion and the primordial religion – the universal and particular traits" (pp. 15–40).

53. An interesting contribution to the discussion on the background of the question-and-answer format as used in religious instruction (with references to Pijper, Huizinga, etc.) is made by A. van Selms, *'N Tweetalige (Arabiese en Afrikaanse) Kategismus* (Amsterdam: Noord-Hollandsche Uitg. Mij., 1951), pp. 25–28.

54. Van Selms, in the publication just mentioned, sees this double answer as a "compromise," since he assumes that there is a constant tension between reason and revelation in all religions; ibid., p. 30.

55. Kenneth Cragg, *The Call of the Minaret* (New York: Oxford University Press, 1956), p. 67; cf. also p. 69, "Small conjunctions often carry profound significance. There is none more tremendous than that which links the One God with the human instrument of His revelation and His will, in the creed and devotion of Islam."

56. This sura is often described as containing the essence of the whole Quranic message. See also S. 42:11 and numerous verses that emphasize the incomparability of Him "other than Whom there is none" – in many instances in the language of praise and thanksgiving; S. 2:255; 3:2; 24:35; 28:70; 59:22–24; 68:13 and passim.

57. A terminology used in several passages dealing with the polytheists (for example, S. 6:100–101; 16:57, 62; 17:40; 37:149, 152, 153; 43:16–18; 52:39; 53:21–22; 72:3), as well as in the context of a criticism of a notion current among Christians (4:171, 172; 2:116, 19:35).

58. A clause occurring in this form twenty-four times, with the variants "no God but I" in S. 16:2; 20:14; 21:25; "no God but Thee" in S. 21:87; and "besides Whom there is no God" and "no God besides Allah" in S. 9:31; 20:98; 37:35; 38:65; 47:19; 59:22, 23.

59. A notion not unknown from their own tradition to many Western polemicists who interpreted this *in the case of Islam and the Quran* as "arbitrariness" and "capriciousness." The "whom He wills" language plays no doubt an important role in the Quran, but it is an expression of the freedom of the God in Whom people are called to put their trust and in Whom they are invited to take refuge. The difficulty, clearly, remains to do justice to both the latter aspect and the notion of the sovereign freedom of God. If they are seen in the tension of their interrelatedness, it becomes obvious that there is no justification for a typology of Islam as that given by, for example, Gustav Mensching: "Die Religion des demonischen Willensmacht und der vollkommener Ergebung"; *Vergleichende Religionswissenschaft,* 2nd ed. (Heidelberg: Quelle & Meyer, 1949), pp. 57–59. Although only the second part of this characterization is used in the title of the section on Islam in his later study, *Die Religion* (Stuttgart: C. E. Schwab, 1959), the author's assessment of the Quranic witness of God has not changed, as is evident from the following statement (p. 59): "Dämonische Willensallmacht ist der Gott Mohammeds, eine Willkürwille, von dem alles Lebendige abhängt."

60. In no way is this expression to be treated as a single "prooftext" – the Quran abounds with verses stressing the mercy of God. "The immediate impression from a cursory reading of the Quran is that of the infinite majesty of God and His equally infinite mercy," Fazlur Rahman, *Major Themes of the Qur'ān,* p. 1.

61. "No one can estimate the power of Islam as a religion who does not take into account the love at the heart of it for this figure [the Prophet] . . . the love of this figure is perhaps the strongest binding force in a religion which has so marked a binding power," Constance E. Padwick, *Muslim Devotions. A Study of Prayer Manuals in Common Use* (London: S.P.C.K., 1961), p. 145.

62. Cragg and Speight, *Islam from Within,* pp. 67–70: "Celebrating Muhammad."

63. Also the confidence and assurance that the ultimate triumph and victory are with God, His Messenger and those who obey them, no matter how much other persons and powers may try to extinguish God's Light. See, for example, S. 9:32; 61:8; 58:20–21; 5:56, etc. The pattern of the Noah and all other "punishment" stories will continue to be repeated until the final judgement day.

64. Many have drawn attention to the Quranic language that the decisive choice for all persons, in their response to God, is that between gratitude and ingratitude, S. 14:7; cf. 76:3 and 2:152. Rudi Paret lists at S. 10:12 and 10:22 more than twenty verses dealing with the theme of people's (un)gratefulness in their answer to expressions of God's goodness. See also S. 14:34; 17:67; 22:66; 42:48; 43:15; 80:17 and 100:6, verses listed by Paret at 11:9–10; *Der Koran*

Kommentar und Konkordanz (Stuttgart: W. Kohlhammer, 1971), pp. 218, 220, and 232 respectively.

65. In a variety of ways the Quran describes God's sending of messengers and prophets as an, or perhaps rather as *the*, expression of His mercy; for some references see *Christological Perspectives*, pp. 212–13 and p. 301, notes 97–99.

66. Muḥammad b. Abdallah al-Khatib, *Mishkat al-Masabih* (Lucknow, AH 1319) X, ii, 2, as translated in Margaret Smith, *The Way of the Mystics* (London: Sheldon Press, 1976; first pub. 1931), p. 143.

Glossary[*]

adhān:	Call to prayer.
al-'adl:	Justice; The Just (one of the Names of God).
Allah:	God; lit. The One and Only God: It is both a'descriptor' denoting the object of worship/devotion, and it is the Name of God.
al-āmana:	The trust.
al-'aqīda:	Lit. that which binds; creed, doctrine, belief.
arkān al-dīn:	'The pillars of the faith'; lit. the cornerstones of religion.
al-asmā' al-ḥusnā:	The beautiful Names (of God).
āya:	Lit. sign (as in nature); the smallest unit in which the chapters of the Qur'ān are divided; a verse in the Qur'ān.
bai'a (or *bay'a*):	Pledge; oath of allegiance.
baitullāh al-ḥarām:	The Sanctified House of God.
baraka:	Grace; bounty.
bashariyya:	Humanity; the flesh and blood component of that humanity.
al-bayān:	The Clarification; name given to the Qur'ān.

*This is a compilation of terms which have occurred in the text. It is not intended to be exhaustive.

al-dhikr:	The Remembrance; name given to the Qur'ān.
dīn:	Religion; lit. Way, judgement, debt, loyalty.
farḍ:	Mandatory duty; obligation.
farḍ kifāya: *farḍ 'ayn*:	Collective duty; individual duty; terms used in *fiqh*.
fiqh:	Muslim jurisprudence.
fiṭra:	Created nature; human nature as moulded by its Creator.
al-furqān:	The Standard; Criterion; name given by God to the Qur'ān. Cf. *al-bayān; al-dhikr.*
al-ḥajj:	The pilgrimage to Makka.
al-Ḥaqq:	Truth; The (Source of) Truth; one of the Names of God. Cf. *al-'adl*.
al-ḥarām:	The Sanctuary (not to be confused with *ḥarām*: the forbidden; the unlawful; in sense of that which is beyond trespassing).
al-hudā:	The Guidance.
al-ḥudūd:	Refers to the limits, or the boundaries, which the *sharī'a* (i.e. the Law) sets on human conduct. Beyond these limits actions are conceived as morally and legally incriminating (*ḥarām*/i.e. forbidden). Within them action is morally and legally just (*ḥalāl*/i.e. permissible).
'ibāda:	Worship; devotion.
iḥrām:	Ritual of consecration that accompanies *Ḥajj*.
iḥsān:	The perfection of an act; an act in truth; to excel.
ikhlāṣ:	The purity of intention; sincerity.
īmān:	Faith; belief in faith (not to be confused with *imām*: leader).
istishhād:	Being slain in the way of God; martyrdom.

i'tikāf:	The act of withdrawing from routine activity in self-consecration to spiritual devotion; to go into retreat.
jabal (as in *jabal al-raḥma*):	Mount; mount of Mercy: name of mountain in 'Arafāt. Site of pilgrimage.
jamā'a:	The community, collectively; consensus.
jihād:	Striving in the way of God; self-exertion; struggle.
al-kalima:	The Word; refers to the profession of faith: *lā ilāhā illā Allāh*.
khilāfa:	Vicegerency.
kufr:	Unbelief; lit. ingratitude (opp. *īmān*).
mashhad:	A spectacle; place of witness; an experience vividly witnessed.
mihrāb:	That enclave in the wall of a mosque showing the direction of the *Ka'ba*; niche.
Muḥammad:	Name of the last Prophet and messenger who communicated the Qur'ān; literally, it means 'the one who is ever praised, who gives praise and whose praise resounds'. (Cf. the 'Paraclete'.)
mujāhid:	One who undertakes *jihād*; a volunteer in the righteous strife; connot. of sacrifice, exertion in a just cause.
nafs:	The self; the inner-directed psyche.
nīya:	The intention; intent.
nūr:	Light.
al-qayyim:	That which is of worth and value; the upright. Cf. *al-dīn al-qayyim*.
qibla:	That which one faces; orientation, direction Muslims face in their prayers (i.e. the Ka'ba).

qiyām: The act of keeping/holding vigil in devotion to God; usually refers to spending the night in prayer and recitation of the Qur'ān.

Qur'ān: The Holy Book of Islam; it is the verbatim recording of the last Message of God to man, as it was revealed to the Prophet Muḥammad. Qur'ān, lit. the Recitation, or The Reading; consists of 30 (*juz'*) Parts, each divided into 2 sections, which are further subdivided. The smallest aggregate unit is the *āya,* which are collected in 114 'chapters' or *sūras,* lit. steps, scales); the Qur'ān was revealed over some 22 years (between 610–632 before the Prophet's death, it was recited in its entirety in the order dictated by the archangel Jibrīl (Gabriel). This was different to the chronological order of the individual *āyas* as they came down over the years in their segmented sequence *tanjīm.* For collection and authentication of the Qur'ān, see summary in Appendix 2. Important to note is, historically, the consensus on the Qur'ān. Today, among the 1000 million Muslims there is only One Qur'ān.

Rabb al-'ālamīn: Lord of the worlds; one of the epithets of God.

raḥma: Mercy (cf. *al-Raḥmān* and *al-Raḥīm*: foremost of the Names of God).

rak'a: Unit of ritual prayer.

rasūl-Allāh: The Messenger of God; God's Apostle.

ṣadaqa: Charity, lit. an act of truth (*ṣidq* = truth).

sa'ī: Lit. the purposeful striving; ritually, refers to the trek back and forth between the two hills of Ṣafa and Marwa undertaken by the pilgrim, or the visitor to the Sanctuary. It consecrates the plight – and the reward of

	Hājir, mother of Ismā'īl. (Cf. root H-J-R, as *hijra* denoting emigration and connoting forsaking (of ease, security, etc.) for the sake of God.)
sakīna:	An inner peace; innate state of tranquillity, serenity and contentment
ṣalāh:	Prayers, lit. connection, contact, closeness.
salām:	Peace.
shahāda:	Lit. the act of bearing witness; the confession of Faith; the *kalima*.
sharī'a(h):	Lit. the way/path/brook that leads to the spring-source; refers to the Law; the legal system; the principles and fundamentals of which are drawn from the Qur'ān and the *sunna* (see below).
shirk:	The act of associating others in the worship of God; professing loyalty to other creeds and other ways other than that inscribed by God in the Qur'ān; this is the greatest 'sin' in Islam (opp. *tawḥīd*).
al-sirāṭ ul-mustaqīm:	The Straight Path.
ṣiyām (pl. of *ṣawm*):	Fasting – abstaining from food and drink from dawn to sunset prescribed for the ninth month of the Muslim calendar, Ramaḍān.
sulṭān:	Power; dominance.
Sunna(h):	Qur'ānically, used to designate the ways of Creation; i.e. the laws of the universe, and the laws of society and those who have gone before history; conventional Arabic usage: refers to the beaten path; used in Islamic context, it refers to the Way of the Prophet, his precedent and his example.
takāful:	Mutual responsibility; the practice of Muslim social security and communal mutuality.

taqwā: The act of heeding God in all one's deeds, by refraining from that which provokes His wrath, and engaging in all that invites His favour; God-consciousness that conduces to a positive state of being. This is the cardinal virtue in Islam, where among a universally equal humanity, the noblest in the sight of God are those of the greatest *taqwā*.

taskhīr: Subordination; rendering an object in a state of passive subjection (as with nature vs. man).

ṭawāf: Circumrotation; circumambulation; the act of walking round the Ka'ba seven times reciting prayers and du'ā's, invoking God's mercy and blessings. The ritual greeting extended by the pilgrim to the House of God.

tawḥīd: The act of consecrating the absolute Oneness of God; the unpolluted and undiluted practice of 'monotheism'.

Umma: Qur'ānic designation of the Muslim Community.

'umra: Refers to the visit to the Noble Sanctuary outside the regular season of *Ḥajj* – sometimes called 'the lesser pilgrimage'; unlike *Ḥajj, 'umra* is not mandatory; it is a visit of (spiritual) love and yearning for 'contiguity' with *bayt Allāh al-ḥarām*.

yawm al-dīn: The Day of Judgement.

zakāt (*zakāh*): The poor dues; it is the compulsory payment of a fixed proportion of one's material wealth, annually, to the community. There is no Church in Islam; so the money spent constitutes a fund for social welfare. Its implementation is the responsibility of the State and public organizations.

ẓulm: Injustice (shares same root with 'darkness') cf. *baghī* (excess; trespassing bounds; oppression) and *ṭughyān*/*ṭaghūt* (tyranny).

Select Bibliography

The repertoire on Islam in contemporary scholarship in the West is vast and growing. The modern 'classic' is possibly Marshall G. S. Hodgson, *The Venture of Islam* (Chicago, 1974) in 3 volumes. In a similar vein of scope and scholarship the work by Ira Lapidus, *A History of Islamic Societies* (Cambridge University Press, 1988) constitutes the most recent venture by Western academic scholarship to go beyond conventional Orientalism in an objective survey of Islamic history from 'without'. One of the more readable, balanced and useful overviews of Islamic history and politics which have become popular in the past decade is the volume *Islam: The Religious and Political Life of a World Community* (Praeger, 1984) edited by Marjorie Kelly. Some recent Western scholarship is attempting to see the view from within and set new standards in cross-cultural understanding. John Obert Voll's work belongs to this category. His *Islam: Continuity and Change* (Westview, 1982), a perceptive work on Islam in politics today, is recommended for its auspicious beginnings in this direction. More recently, two general overall concise works include John Esposito's *Islam: The Straight Path* (Oxford University Press, 1988) and Frederick Denny's, *An Introduction to Islam* (Macmillan, 1985). Another promising trend that bodes well for a more positive intra-cultural exchange is the attempt to communicate, unmediated, some of the present trends, in the spate of cultural effervescence in the Muslim World. An example is Yvonne Haddad's, *Contemporary Islam and the Challenge of History* (particularly its annexes) (Albany, New York, 1982).

The greater part of Western scholarship, however, is well publicized and easily accessible. This is why the following selection focuses on authors and writings less likely to be familiar to the average Western audience of Islam. The common factor that these authors share is that they are – generally – all exponents of

Islam from within its belief-system and cultural world-view. In this sense, the selection is a restricted one; it is intended to supplement the ideas put forth in the various essays, and in the work as a whole, including its visual programme. On the other hand, as the purpose of this guide is a practical one, the present selection is further made with an eye on the availability of the suggested readings. Most of the titles mentioned below are available from the Islamic Book Services in Europe and America.

A. The Qur'ān

The following are the recommended English translations/interpretations, alphabetically ordered.

ALI, A. Yusuf, *The Holy Qur'an: Text, Translation and Commentary,* Brentwood, Amana Corp., 1409/1989.

ARBERRY, A. J., *The Koran Interpreted,* London, Allen & Unwin, 1955.

ASAD, M., *The Message of the Qur'an:* Translated and Explained, Gibraltar, Dar al-Andalus, 1980.

IRVING, T. B., AHMAD, K. and AHSAN, M. M., *The Qur'ān: Basic Teachings,* Leicester, The Islamic Foundation, 1979.

MAWDŪDĪ, S. A. A., *Towards Understanding the Qur'ān,* 3 vols, Leicester, The Islamic Foundation, 1988–90.

PICKTHALL, M. M., *The Meaning of the Glorious Qur'an,* New York, New American Library, 1953.

B. General

ABDALATI, H., *Islam in Focus,* Indianapolis, American Trust Publications, 1975.

ABDUL-LATIF, S., *The Mind al Quran Builds,* Lahore, Accurate Printers.

AHMAD, K. (ed.), *Islam: Its Meaning and Message,* Leicester, The Islamic Foundation, 1976.

ARGUS COMMUNICATIONS, *The Islamic Tradition,* Argus, Texas, Religion in Human Culture, World Religions Curriculum Development Center, 1978.

ASAD, M., *Islam at the Crossroads,* Gibraltar, Dar al-Andalus, 1982.

——, *The Road to Mecca,* New York, Simon & Schuster, 1954/Gibraltar, Dar al-Andalus, 1978.

AZZAM, A. R., *The Eternal Message of Muhammad,* London and New York, Quartet Books, 1979.

BAMATE, H., *Muslim Contribution to Civilization,* Geneva, Islamic Centre.

BENNABI, M., *The Qur'anic Phenomenon,* Indianapolis, American Trust Publications, 1983.

BROHI, A. K., *The Qur'ān and its Impact on Human History,* Leicester, The Islamic Foundation, 1979.

BUCAILLE, M., *The Bible, the Qur'an and Science: The Holy Scriptures Examined in the Light of Modern Knowledge,* Fifth edition, revised and expanded, Paris, Seghers, 1987/Indianapolis, American Trust Publications, 1979.

BURKHARDT, T., *Art of Islam, Language and Meaning,* World of Islam Festival Trust, 1976.

EATON, Gai, *Islam and the Destiny of Man,* State University of New York Press/Islamic Texts Society, 1985.

AL-FARUQI, I. R., *Atlas of Islam,* Niles Ill., Argus Communications, 1979.

——, *Tawhīd: Its Meaning and Implications,* Washington, DC, The International Institute of Islamic Thought, 1984.

AL-FARUQI, L., *Women, Muslim Society and Islam,* Indianapolis, American Trust Publications, 1988.

AL-GHAZĀLĪ, *Inner Dimensions of Islamic Worship,* trans. by Muhtar Holland, Leicester, The Islamic Foundation, 1983.

HAMIDULLAH, M., *Introduction to Islam,* London, 1979.

HAYKAL, M. H., *Life of Muhammad,* trans. by I. R. Faruqi, Indianapolis, American Trust Publications, 1985.

IRVING, T. B., *Islam and Social Responsibility,* Leicester, The Islamic Foundation, 1980.

——, 'Terms and Concepts: Problems in Translating the Qur'an' in: K. Ahmad and Z. I. Ansari (eds.), *Islamic Perspectives: Studies in Honour of Sayyid Abul A'lā Mawdūdī,* Leicester, The Islamic Foundation, 1979/1399.

JAMEELAH, M., *Islam and Western Society,* Lahore, Muhammad Yusuf Khan & Sons, 1984.

EL-KIRDANY, A. A. S., *Glimpses of the Scientific Unattainable Marvels in the Qur'an,* selected and translated from the late Dr. M. A. El-Ghamrawy, Cairo, 1977.

MANNAN, M. A., *Islamic Economics, Theory and Practice,* Lahore, Shaikh Muhammad Ashraf, 1970.

MAWDŪDĪ, S. A. A., *Finality of Prophethood,* Lahore, Islamic Publications Ltd., 1975.

——, *Jihad in Islam,* Lahore, Islamic Publications Ltd., 1976.

——, *A Short History of the Revivalist Movement in Islam,* Lahore, Islamic Publications Ltd., 1963, 1972, (revised) 1976.

——, *Towards Understanding Islam,* Leicester, The Islamic Foundation, 1980.

——, *Witnesses unto Mankind: The Purpose and Duty of the Muslim Ummah,* ed. and trans. by Khurram Murad, Leicester, The Islamic Foundation, 1986/1406.

MAY, D., 'Women in Islam' in: C. K. Pullapilly (ed.), *Islam in the Contemporary World,* Notre Dame, 1980.

MORGAN, K. (ed.), *Islam, the Straight Path: Islam Interpreted by Muslims,* New York, Ronald Press, 1958.

MURAD, K. J., *Way to the Qur'ān,* Leicester, The Islamic Foundation, 1985, 1990 (revised).

NASR, S. H., *Ideals and Realities of Islam,* London, Allen & Unwin, 1966.

——, *Islam and the Plight of Modern Man,* Longman, 1975.

——, *Science and Civilization in Islam,* Cambridge, Harvard University Press, 1968.

PICKTHALL, M. M., *The Cultural Side of Islam,* Delhi, The Islamic Book Trust, 1982.

QUTB, S., *In the Shade of the Qur'an,* Vol. 30*, London, Muslim Welfare House, 1979.

——, *Islam – The Religion of the Future,* Kuwait, International Islamic Federation of Student Organizations, 1971.

——, *Islam and Universal Peace,* Indianapolis, American Trust Publications, 1977.

——, *Milestones,* Kuwait, International Islamic Federation of Student Organizations, 1980.

——, *This Religion of Islam,* Kuwait, International Islamic Federation of Student Organizations, 1977.

RAHMAN, F., *Islam,* Chicago and London, 1979.

ROBERTS, R., *The Social Laws of the Qur'an,* London, Curzon Press, 1925, reprinted 1977.

SARDAR, Z., *Islamic Futures,* London, Mansell Publications, 1985.

SCHOUN, F., *Understanding Islam,* trans. from German, London, Allen & Unwin, 1972.

SHARIF, M. M., *In Search of Truth,* Lahore, Institute of Islamic Centre, 1966.

---

*This is the English translation of one of 30 volumes of an Arabic interpretation of the Qur'ān composed by the author while in prison. Syed Qutb was convicted and eventually executed by a court martial for his beliefs. He is consequently known as 'al-shahid' (martyr of the faith) and is honoured by his followers in line with a tradition of intellectual martyrs in the Islamic tradition.

———, *Studies in Aesthetics,* Lahore, Institute of Islamic Centre, 1964.

SIDDIQI, M., *The Qur'anic Concept of History,* Islamabad, Islamic Research Institute, 1964.

SIDDIQUI, A. H., *A Philosophical Interpretation of History,* Lahore, Idara Nashriyat Islam, n.d.

———, *Selections from Hadith,* Islamic Book Publishers, n.d.

———, *Theocracy and the Islamic State,* London, Islamic Centre, Regents Park, n.d.

SOLIMAN, A. M., *Scientific Trends in the Qur'an,* London, Ta-Ha Publishers, 1985/1406.

SURTY, M. I. H. I., *The Qur'ānic Concept of al-Shirk* (Polytheism), London, Ta-Ha Publishers, revised edition, 1990.

Index